MAGDALENA

Mother · Feminist · Catholic · Latina
stories and reflections

Madeline Ruiz de la Vara Olea

For permission, email Madeline Olea at
magdalena.memoir@gmail.com

ISBN 13: 978-1720360179
ISBN: 10: 1720360170

Printed by CreateSpace, Charleston SC

To my children

Michael, Vincent, Stephanie, Christopher, Margaret

And my grandchildren

Heather, Andrew, Sarah, Vance

With all my love

CONTENTS

PREFACE

It was not my intent to write a memoir or autobiography. That's for someone already in the limelight; whose life or experiences or profession is already interesting to some segment of the population. My life, I felt, was pretty ordinary and I was not into genealogy and really didn't care who begat whom on my ancestral tree.

Yet, I often thought about writing down my family history, mainly because I wanted to preserve my grandmother's (Nani's) stories. Over the years, I compared my memory of these stories with those of my sister and cousins, calling on collective memory to ensure their accuracy. In the process, I realized we had our own stories to share and fantasized having a written record to hand down to the generations after us so they would know who we were. But I had no clue how or where to start.

In 2009, a severe anxiety reaction to pain medication sent me to a psychologist. In the course of therapy, my psychologist suggested I look at baby pictures of myself; photos taken of the real *me*, before environmental factors had had their effect. She said some people gain insight into their inner self through the exercise. I tried but, frankly, I didn't see anything. I did note that I looked sad in my photos, but nothing significant.

As I studied my pictures, it hit me that I knew very little about my birth and early childhood. I had so many questions about what was going on around me before, during and after my birth – where did we live, where did my father work, was I an easy or difficult baby, what were my parents' goals and dreams? Ah, I thought, I can do that for my children. I can write their birth stories.

And so it began. I wrote Michael's birth story, beginning with how his dad and I met. It was a personal story, written for him. And the four others followed. The birth stories describe my children's births, their personalities, and the family circumstances that surrounded them and influenced their development. My focus was on events that occurred before they would have memories of them, but occasionally I refer to something in their later years. Without intending it, the five birth stories present a pretty complete history of my early married life.

In 2010, I mailed the five stories to my children. Their response was gratifying. Not only were they appreciative of my efforts and enjoyed the stories; they asked for more. And so, with a little experience under my belt, I wrote my childhood story, beginning with ancestors I never knew and ending when I met my husband. I sent my childhood story to my siblings and cousins for Christmas, 2011, noting that I loved the idea that someday a great-great-grandchild (not yet a twinkle in anyone's eye) might pick up these stories and learn (perhaps appreciate) a little of their family history. But I wasn't done. I needed to give my grandchildren their birth stories. I did so in the form of letters, which they received on their birthdays in 2012.

At this point, I was not sure what I would do with my finished product. I thought of giving each family member a binder containing the stories. Or, if I could afford it, have the stories bound in some fancy way at our local print shop. I put that aside as a decision to be made in the future.

When I finished the stories that reflected family history, I realized someone could read these stories and still not know who I really am – what I think, what I believe, what makes me uniquely me. If I wanted my children, grandchildren, and descendants to know *me*, then I'd have to write it down. Over the next five years, I offered opinions on work and education and wrote reflections on topics of importance to me: domestic violence, my relationship with the Catholic Church, political activism, mental illness, death. Neither the stories nor the reflections were easy to write. The process was painful and agonizingly slow as I took myself back in time, deep into my psyche, and relived all those memories. There were good memories, of course, but many took me back to sad and difficult times and some reminded me of my failures as a parent and as a daughter. I cried as I wrote them and I cry every time I read them. Yet, I had to be brutally honest, even when the truth came with anguish. It was a cathartic experience, to be sure, and with it came some measure of peace and understanding and reconciliation.

I was surprised initially when friends and relatives who read pieces of my writings shared that I had awakened deep memories and emotions from their own life experiences; that they had been touched at a very personal level. It was then I realized these were not my stories alone. Life experiences are universal – birth and death, health and illness, joy and tragedy – they transcend culture and ethnicity and generation. I was charmed that what brought me peace and understanding and reconciliation could do the same for a friend and, perhaps, for a total stranger.

Because my manuscript was completed over an eight-year period and because most stories and reflections stand on their own, the reader will find some repetition of events or thoughts. I have tried to eliminate duplication when not necessary to the piece, but at times it is inevitable. For example, Stephanie's birth story was completed in 2009, but my reflection on Stephanie was written six years later. The former piece tells what was happening *with her* right after birth; the latter relates what was happening *within me* as I struggled with her disabilities.

Another issue that needs some explaining is the fact that my letters to grandchildren Heather and Andrew are fewer than half the number of pages as my letters to grandchildren Sarah and Vance. Please don't misconstrue this to reflect anything negative in my relationship to my older two grandchildren. I love them all equally and have wonderful memories of all their childhoods. However, Sarah and Vance lived with me for almost two years and this alone accounts for more stories in my letters to them.

As I read sections of this final manuscript, I recognize the extent to which I place my mother in an unfavorable light (my daughter will undoubtedly do the same with me some day). I wrote about one side of my mother – the side that struggled with fears and anxiety her entire life. The other side is a remarkably intelligent woman with strong convictions; a feminist and health food advocate before it was fashionable, who would drop what she was doing if you needed help and move heaven and earth to fix whatever problem was in the way. She wanted more for her children than she had, and she lived to see it.

This is an honest depiction of a real family (only my ex-husband's name has been changed and I am deliberately vague about my current area of residence). The opinions offered and the lens through which I view the past are mine alone.

I use three surnames as the author because this is a family story and the names represent my entire family: my mother is Ruiz, my father is de la Vara, and my children are Olea. A side note: my father changed the spelling of his name to Dela Vara after he was disowned by his family. I used his spelling until high school when a teacher insisted that de la Vara was the correct spelling for my name.

I am not a scholar or an intellectual. This is a simply-written narrative of my life experiences. If you find yourself in a story or a thought touches your heart, I could not ask for more.

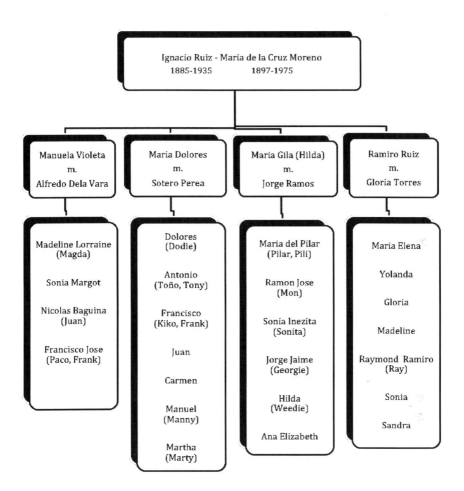

Ignacio Ruiz - Maria de la Cruz Moreno
1885-1935   1897-1975

| Manuela Violeta m. Alfredo Dela Vara | Maria Dolores m. Sotero Perea | María Gila (Hilda) m. Jorge Ramos | Ramiro Ruiz m. Gloria Torres |

Madeline Lorraine (Magda)

Sonia Margot

Nicolas Baguina (Juan)

Francisco Jose (Paco, Frank)

Dolores (Dodie)

Antonio (Toño, Tony)

Francisco (Kiko, Frank)

Juan

Carmen

Manuel (Manny)

Martha (Marty)

Maria del Pilar (Pilar, Pili)

Ramon Jose (Mon)

Sonia Inezita (Sonita)

Jorge Jaime (Georgie)

Hilda (Weedie)

Ana Elizabeth

Maria Elena

Yolanda

Gloria

Madeline

Raymond Ramiro (Ray)

Sonia

Sandra

I

LA FAMILIA

All I know about my birth is what's in my birth certificate, which I saw for the first time when I was about 35. Some of it was expected: born in Douglas, Arizona on August 10, 1940 at 3:00 pm. Some of it was interesting: my mother (Manuela Violeta Ruiz aka Mom) was in the hospital 10 minutes before I was born and at full term, I weighed 5 lbs. 1 oz. Some of it was downright shocking: my name was not what I'd always believed it was.

Until I started school, I was called Magda but when I entered first grade, Mom enrolled me as Madeline. This was supposedly my legal name but Mom was somewhat apologetic. The explanation over the years varied but mostly it went like this: the person who took the information from Mom for the birth certificate got my name wrong and put down Madeline. Indeed, that is the name on my hospital birth record. However, what Mom had really intended to name me was never clear. Sometimes she seemed to apologize for not spelling my name *Madeleine*. She thought the French spelling was much more elegant. The one fact that was clear as I was growing up was that Madeline was a very unlikely name for a Mexican-American girl residing in a primarily Spanish-speaking neighborhood. People looked at me rather oddly when I gave them my name. *Me llamo Madeline?*

In my 30's, I had an opportunity to go to Mexico as a translator for a group called The Flying Samaritans. They set up clinics in poor, remote villages to provide medical and dental exams and screenings. I needed my birth certificate and Mom offered to get it for me. When it arrived, you can imagine my surprise to see that my legal name was Magdalena. That's more like it. *Me llamo Magdalena.* I loved my newly-discovered name – it felt like the real me. I've never said (or written about) this but, to this day, I feel awkward when I say *Madeline* out loud.   In my heart, I am *Magdalena.*

After I was born, we lived in Douglas for about 2½ years, in a little house close to my grandmother (Maria de la Cruz Moreno aka Nani), aunts Dolores Ruiz (aka Lola) and Maria Gila Ruiz (aka Hilda), and uncle Ramiro Ruiz. When I was born, Lola was 16, Hilda was almost 11 and Ramiro was 8. I was probably spoiled by the family and Hilda always thought I was special – like a doll just for her to play with.

I never met my dad's (Alfredo Dela Vara, aka Pops) family, however, even though they all lived in Douglas. They had disowned my father when he and Mom became engaged, didn't attend the wedding, and never tried to meet me or my siblings. We will never know what happened to cause such a severe rift; the explanations were never consistent.   Some implied that my mother was overly coquettish; others, that my father was expected to contribute to the family income and not marry so young.   The cloud of secrecy, mystery, anger, resentment, and curiosity hung over the family all my life. Pops gave up his family for the woman he loved and only sought out his brothers and sister after Mom passed away. By then, no one had a sliver of a memory as to exactly what had robbed me of significant relatives.   It was a large family – I had two grandparents, six uncles, one aunt and a slew of cousins who weren't part of my life.

2

My maternal grandfather, Ignacio Ruiz, was 12 years older than Nani and she boasted about his green eyes and ruddy complexion. They were both born in Mexico (he in the State of Sinaloa, she in Bacadehuachi, Sonora) but they met in Douglas where they lived at the time. They were married in 1917 at Immaculate Conception Church when he was 31 or 32 and she was 19 or 20. Ignacio was a carpenter by trade but was also active in local politics. Sometimes, that included going against the establishment and landing in jail, much to Nani's displeasure.

Ignacio and Nani moved easily between Agua Prieta, Sonora and Douglas, Aizona and Mom was born in Agua Prieta. She always said her father felt strongly that she should be born in Mexico, although the reason for this was never clarified. A travel permit issued April 17, 1919, has a picture of Nani holding Mom at age 6 months and shows them residing in Agua Prieta. The permit allowed daily travel between Agua Prieta and Douglas "to make purchases."

Lola was born in Bacadehuachi where Nani's parents lived. According to Lola's personal memoirs, her father was hired to build a school for the town and the family stayed with Nani's parents. Nani was already pregnant with Lola so she was born there. In her memoirs, Lola described her grandmother as short, slim and very quiet.

There is no question that Ignacio was the adventurous one and Nani was the stable one. He got his way initially but by the time Nani was pregnant with Hilda she put her foot down and refused to move again. There's even the possibility that she packed up her kids and returned to the U.S. on her own during one of Ignacio's politically motivated incarcerations. Anyway, Hilda and Ramiro were both born in Douglas, delivered by a local midwife as all the children had been.

Mom and Pops, as it turned out, were born in different countries but a very short distance apart; in fact, the distance between Douglas and Agua Prieta is only 3.4 miles. I suspect that Nani and my grandfather mostly walked back and forth and did most of their shopping on the U.S side. Pops never talked about his family crossing the border into Mexico so, obviously, there was no need to go the other way.

Mom was only 17 when her father died at the age of 50. According to his death certificate, my grandfather was diagnosed with the flu on Dec. 2, 1935 and was hospitalized at Cochise County Hospital. Three days later he was diagnosed with pneumonia and died on Dec. 10. Nani told me the story endless times, always with tears in her eyes and guilt in her heart. She said she was by his bedside during the day but had to leave him at night to tend to her children. One night, he became delirious with fever and ran out of the hospital into the cold air. He died before she returned to the hospital the next morning. (If only she had stayed with him, she later cried....)

Nani had never worked out of the home and Ramiro was only 3 years old when my grandfather died. Nani told me she took in laundry and sewing and my sister Sonia heard stories of her selling her good clothes and jewelry, including a beautiful coat with a fur collar. That wasn't enough to support a family of five so Mom, who had plans to attend the local university, was forced to quit high school and get a job.

Mom must have mourned her father's death on many levels. Her academic goals and career dreams were crushed as she went from carefree student to responsible adult overnight. And, she lost a parent who had indulged and probably pampered her all her life. Indeed, she cherished memories of being held and carried by her father as a child. But Mom wasn't alone in longing for her father. According to my cousins, Lola and Hilda never stopped mourning him.

Sometime between my second and third birthdays, Pops came to California in search of a job and a new beginning for the family. He found work at the shipyards in San Pedro and then brought Mom and me to Los Angeles. For a few weeks or months, we either stayed with *Tia Amelia* (Nani's sister-in-law) or rented an apartment (or both) across the street from Hollenbeck Park in Boyle

Heights. We loved that park and spent a lot of time there. A typical weekend outing for families was a blanket on the grass under a shady tree; the mom spreading her packed lunch; the dad throwing the ball; the kids begging for a walk to the lake. Except, we were fortunate to live so close that our park excursions were not limited to the weekend.

In a short time, we were able to rent a little house on Fickett Street, right next to Hollenbeck Jr. High School. I don't know why Pops picked Boyle Heights to live in since it is about 30 miles from San Pedro where he worked. There were no freeways then and that was a long drive. We must not have had a car at first because I remember Pops being dropped off at the curb and my running with open arms to meet him.

I only have snatches of memories of life in that house. I entertained myself by watching the Jr. High School kids in their playground. I'd sit on the ground, nose pressed against the chain link fence as the young teens exercised or played games during gym class. I also played with the children who lived next door, always under the watchful eye of Mom who was sure we were up to no good. And she might have been right because I remember the little boy chasing me and trying to wet me with a stream of pee. That was when I first learned that boy and girl anatomies differed and, frankly, I was quite horrified.

I think there were also dark moments in that little house on Fickett Street. Mom was extremely lonely without her family and Pops was out of the house most of the day. One of my most vivid memories was that of Mom and Pops arguing and then Mom holding me at the kitchen sink, wiping blood off my forehead. She and I were both crying. A dish had broken and a small fragment had cut me. When Mom tried to explain the incident many, many years later, she couldn't get the words out. Then, and at many other times, she simply said, *"Tu no sabes, mi hijita."* She was right, I didn't know – then or to this day.

When Mom got pregnant with my sister, Sonia, Pops took us back to Douglas. The explanation was that Mom was sick and Nani needed to take care of her. My guess is that she was suffering from depression and Pops didn't want to leave her home alone all day. He left Mom and me with Nani and returned to LA to work. I don't remember anything about Nani's house but I do remember waiting for the postman because Pops would often send me comic books in the mail. I also know Mom sent him photos of me because I found one in which she points out I had learned to play hopscotch.

This wasn't Mom's first bout with depression. She often told the story of being sick when she was two years old. She was listless and didn't want to eat or play. The doctor told Nani and my grandfather to dress and surround her in red and to give in to her every wish, no matter what it was or what time of day or night. I don't know whether she remembered any of it or simply remembered being told about it, but she said her father carried her constantly and took her for rides in the middle of the night. The story seemed to give her great comfort and had significant meaning for her as she retold it throughout her life.

Sonia was born in Douglas on March 10, 1945 when I was 4 ½ years old. I have only a snapshot in my head of Pops' car pulling into the driveway with my new baby sister. That summer, Pops bought a piece of property for $4,000 at 719 So. Mott Street in Boyle Heights, right around the corner from the house on Fickett Street. There were two houses on the lot – the front house (for my immediate family) had two bedrooms and one bath; the back house (for my extended family) had one bedroom and one bath. It was a poor but well-maintained neighborhood occupied primarily by families of Mexican origin but sprinkled lightly with Russian immigrants in their orthodox attire. Whittier Blvd. was just half a block away from the house, with direct streetcar access to downtown Los Angeles. Brooklyn Ave. was also nearby, with its Jewish culture and fabulous bakeries. And, of course, the Latin influence was everywhere, from *tortillerias* to *pachucos*.

We moved by train to LA in June, 1945. There was no room for the entire family to travel at the same time because the trains were carrying many soldiers, so Mom, Sonia, Lola and I came first and Nani, Hilda and Ramiro followed the next day. We were on Pullman cars that converted from seats during the day to beds at night, with curtains that closed for privacy. I clearly remember how exciting it was and how cozy it felt and how happy we all were. I don't remember the soldiers but Hilda, who was 15 at the time, remembered them well.

That fall, I started kindergarten at the local public school. It was a three-block walk down Whittier Blvd. to Euclid Avenue School. Pops may have driven us sometimes but I remember Mom walking me to school and us stopping at the Kress across from the school. The S.H. Kress & Co., a quintessential five and dime retail chain that closed in the early '80s, was a magical place – with rows of notions and goodies as far as the eye could see. As I was fantasizing about all the candy and toys, Mom was picking out patterns, fabric and thread for the next outfit she would sew.

Mom and I would also stop at the drug store, kitty-corner from the school. I loved that store with its soda fountain and pharmacy and all sorts of medicinal products. It had a very particular drug store smell – part menthol, part root beer float – that permeated the senses and instantly promoted a feeling of calm and wellness.

The happy times did not last long, however. Soon after I started school (perhaps a few weeks), I got the measles. I spent days on my parents' bed with the curtains drawn so that the room was very dark. There was no television then but I had coloring books and crayons. I didn't return to school after I recovered, possibly because Mom feared further illnesses, or perhaps she wasn't up to the walk every day. There was also an incident that alarmed us. Another girl in my class was accused of stealing some small item and the teacher pulled up her dress and searched her in front of the other children. I'm sure I was traumatized and Mom was equally appalled as I told her the story, so that may have been the reason my early education was cut short.

The summer before my 6th birthday, I got hit with another childhood illness. This time Sonia and I both got the whooping cough. What a miserable time for poor Mom. Sonia did the typical whooping cough thing – she whooped – yes, a terrible sound as she drew breath between coughs, but at least she could breathe. I, on the other hand, couldn't catch my breath between coughs and I remember Mom frantically fanning me with a newspaper as I jumped and waved my arms in panic because the breath just would not come. Between the two of us, we kept Mom hopping, especially when we coughed at the same time. It seems to me, we were sick for a long time – it felt like the whole summer. I suppose that can't be but I do remember the family going to Seal Beach a lot because the ocean air seemed to help. All my life, I've gone through periods of spasmodic coughing and Mom always believed it stemmed from that awful whooping cough.

When Sonia was a baby, she had a medical emergency of her own. A high fever made her go limp and she appeared to stop breathing. Someone called Dr. Avitia, a chiropractor with a practice a couple of blocks up Whittier Blvd. He came quickly and wrapped her in a blanket to "sweat the fever out." I didn't understand what was happening but I took my cues from Hilda who was crying softly in the corner of the room. I was crying too when Dr. Avitia came over and gently told us she was going to be all right.

When I started first grade, Hilda was a sophomore at Our Lady Queen of Angels Elementary and High School. OLQA was about five miles from the house and a stone's throw from downtown Los Angeles, near China Town. It was the school attached to the old Plaza Church (Cathedral of Our Lady of the Angels) near Olvera Street. Our local parish (Our Lady of the Rosary of Talpa) didn't have a school attached to it and it was decided I would also attend OLQA. Hilda and I took the R Car (streetcar) to 7th and Broadway and then transferred to a bus that dropped us off 1 ½ blocks from the school. The streetcar and bus rides were our regular routine but Pops sometimes drove us to school since he worked evening shifts.

Hilda and I had many exciting moments during our commute to and from school, but two especially come to mind. One morning on our way to school, Hilda and a large group of schoolmates that

8

rode the same bus got off at our appointed stop. She was chatting with her friends and wasn't aware that I had been daydreaming and failed to get off the bus with her. When she noticed I was missing, she took the following bus, explaining the situation to the bus driver who hurried to catch up with the bus carrying me. At the same time, I awoke from my daydream and told my bus driver what happened. He gave me a transfer and explained what I should do to backtrack to my stop. Eventually, Hilda and I had a tearful reunion and that experience became a "remember when..." story for the rest of our lives.

On another occasion, we were on the streetcar on our way home. I was on the window side of the seat and Hilda was sitting behind me with a friend. A man sat next to me and, within minutes, his hand was on my lap. I was terrified but I calmly turned around and asked Hilda if our stop was coming up soon. I wanted the man to know I wasn't alone. She answered me impatiently that it was and I got up and stood next to her. I remember holding my breath as I crossed in front of him to get out of the seat. I don't know that I ever told Hilda or Mom what had happened.

In 1946, Mom applied to become a U.S. citizen. I have no idea why she was unable to complete the process at that time. Over the years, she gave different responses as to why she hadn't become a citizen: her father had expressly wanted her to be born in Mexico; she wanted to own land in Mexico some day; she was displeased that she had to "renounce" her country of origin as she pledged allegiance to her new one. At any rate, Mom did not become a citizen until shortly before she died. Nani, on the other hand, became a citizen when I was a young girl.

My brother, Juan, was born on September 11, 1948, a month after I turned eight. His legal name was Nicolas Baguina – the middle name a tribute to a parish priest. However, we called him Juan from birth and even his social security card showed him as Juan N. B. Dela Vara. My memory of this is that Mom had received lots of hand-me-downs from her sisters and she referred to these as "*juanes*," hence the nickname Juan. He was a delightful baby, the tiniest bit chubby but adorable, and we enjoyed his antics as evidenced by the ton of photos taken of him. That was a happy time for all of us.

II

NANI

When I think about happy times, I think of Nani. We frequently walked to church together and she was oh so pleased when people thought she was my mother. During May, the little girls in our parish wore white dresses and veils and took part in a procession to crown the Blessed Virgin. I remember it as a daily event during the week for the whole month, but it might have been only on designated days. As I walked to church with Nani, we picked colorful flowers from our neighbors' front yards and arrived at church with a beautiful bouquet.

Colorful gardens in the front yard were common in our neighborhood. Nani tended our garden with meticulous care – planting, weeding and watering. In the summer, Sonia and I donned our bathing suits and, as she watered, she was happy to hose us down or put the sprinklers on for us to play in. Nani most certainly had a green thumb and her sweet pea and carnations were my very favorite. She also had a vegetable garden in the back yard and I remember the corn that was as tall as she was.

Then there were the chickens and that mean rooster that seemed to come out of nowhere to chase and torture me. Nani finally had to get rid of him (maybe we ate him!). The image of Nani

11

chasing chickens around the yard is still vivid in my mind. She'd snap their necks and the chickens would run around for a while without their heads. I don't remember her using any tools but I'm sure my eyes were closed throughout the ordeal so I'm not sure. Then she plucked and cooked the chicken and that evening the family enjoyed a tasty dinner, maybe *aroz con pollo* or *caldo*. She was a way tougher woman than I'll ever be!

Nani was my refuge when I wanted to get away from home and I felt most secure when I was around her. Her little house smelled good and the radio was always on to a Mexican station. The lively, ranchera music was infectious and, from an early age, I immediately recognized my favorite singer, Jorge Negrete. As soon as he came on, I crouched in front of the large, stand-alone radio to listen intently. When I was around five years old, my parents took me to a local park where Jorge was performing live and, when people close to the stage got rowdy and a near-riot broke out, some man picked me up, put me on his shoulders, and called out to Jorge that there was a little girl who wanted to see him. He came to the front of the stage and looked out into the crowd but I'm not sure he really saw me.

Nani nourished me both emotionally and physically. I frequently had breakfast at her house because Mom was not feeling well and Nani was already up making breakfast for Lola, Hilda and Ramiro. Usual breakfast fare was *avena* (oatmeal) and a glass of milk with a little coffee just to take the chill off. Unfortunately, by the time I was in high school, I'd get a terrible headache if I didn't have some coffee in the morning. Still, sitting at her kitchen table was one of my favorite things. I loved watching her make tortillas and marveled at how nimbly she twirled the tortilla around as it grew bigger and bigger. I think she enjoyed watching me watch her. Nothing describes the taste of freshly-made tortillas with butter. I also loved how she trimmed her meat and then fried the fat to make crispy *chicharrones*.

It turns out my siblings and cousins all share memories of Nani's tortillas. We also grew up loving two special dishes, thinking

12

they originated with our mothers but now speculating they may have started with Nani. These dishes were *squishies* and *sopitas* (or, in the case of my children, chip with egg). *Squishies* were handmade corn tortillas to which cheese was immediately added and then squeezed by hand (Mom used a kitchen towel to protect her hands) so that tortilla and cheese melded together. *Sopitas* were store-bought corn tortillas torn into small pieces and toasted in a pan to which beaten eggs were added. Both dishes could be enhanced with various spices or other ingredients but these were the basic recipes and, to this day, just thinking about them brings smiles to our faces.

Christmas also brought a smile to my face. Before Lola and Hilda got married, they and Mom and Nani made tamales for the holidays, always a joyous occasion. I remember the happy chatter and the many varieties of tamales they made, including sweet ones with raisins. Menudo was for New Year's and, in later years, it became a Pops specialty. Santa came at Nani's house where we spent Christmas Eve. I always got what I asked for from Santa – and sometimes a little bit extra – so there was no doubt in my mind that Santa existed because I knew my parents could not afford such things.

Nani loved telling stories about her life. It's interesting to me now that I would be her audience because I was never that well versed in Spanish. I certainly understood her and could acknowledge her statements, but it's not like we carried on a running conversation. Nani had one sister, Loretto, and six brothers. Loretto was fair-skinned and a real beauty who took great care to stay out of the sun to protect her skin. I got the impression she was the pampered one in the family. Nani, on the other hand, was more the tomboy - active outdoors and in the sun. She was also the responsible one, spending hours washing her brothers' clothes in the river with handmade soap and starch and then carefully ironing all those shirts.

Life, as it sometimes does, took its own turn with the two sisters. Loretto married a, shall we say, irresponsible rancher and had a rough life as she worked the fields, tended the sheep, and raised her children. She aged quickly and pictures show her looking hard, with skin like weathered leather. Nani, however, kept a youthful, soft and gentle look about her.

One of Loretto's daughters, Julia, remained close to Mom, Lola and Hilda. When I was about 13, my family drove to Tecate to see Julia who had just given birth to a son. I'll never forget that trip. We arrived at a barren lot that accommodated several dwellings and an outhouse. I say dwellings rather than houses because the one-room structures looked like they had been built by hand with glue and had windows but no glass or screens and dirt floors. I had never seen such squalor and could hardly get my mind around the fact that a relative of mine could live like this. Still, I couldn't get away from it because there, in the filth, lay Julia and her sick baby. I was physically repelled.

We were only in Tecate a couple of days, but Mom and Pops took Julia and the baby to the doctor and bought food, clothing, baby products, and medicine. They may have done more that I don't remember, but I do remember the long and sad drive home. The experience left its mark on me. That was the first time – but not the last – that I brooded over the consequences of poverty in the world.

Except for washing and ironing their shirts, Nani didn't tell me much about her brothers. However, a nephew of Nani's, Pablo Moreno, left us the following written history: Ramon fought and died in the Mexican Revolutionary War under Porfirio Diaz; Jose Jesus was a postal administrator and, later, a high ranking military official who was taken prisoner and then shot by a rifle squad; Pablo, a carpenter, was a pacifist and self-taught in the law; Jose Mateo became despondent and disappeared when he found his wife with another man; Maximiliano married Amelia (a flamboyant, loquacious woman whom I remember) and the cause of his death is unknown; Eulalio moved to Los Angeles (possibly with a man) and was either murdered or committed suicide.

Nani told stories of premature births and miscarriages but I don't know how many there were. It was a fairly common occurrence at that time but that didn't lessen the pain. I think most of these babies were boys and included Ramiro. She'd put out her hand, palm up, to show me how little the babies were and talked about keeping them warm by the oven. She especially grieved over one baby – a son named Nachito after his father and with his father's green eyes. With tears in her eyes, Nani described Nachito as robust and full of life until his death around his second birthday. My guess is that he died during a flu epidemic. Nani and Mom both talked about epidemics in which whole families would be found dead in their homes, the front doors wide open.

Another of Nani's often-told stories was that of a young boy in her family who was captured by the Apaches and raised as one of them, most likely for labor. His parents searched for him many years but in vain. When he was older, a man recognized him in a store and traded some supplies (perhaps a wagon) for him. The boy, who had evidence on his head and back of severe beatings, was then reunited with his family. I couldn't remember the details of this tale and got willing help from my cousins who had also grown up with the story.

Another story, as told by Hilda, involved Nani's parents. My great-grandparents went to a 3-day wedding in *Nacosari* and on their return home to *Bacadehuachi*, they were attacked by Apaches. My great-grandfather jumped from his horse onto my great-grandmother's horse and they rode down into a gulch. My great-grandmother's *rebozo* (shawl) was full of holes from the arrows shot by the Indians but, thank goodness for their progeny, neither was hurt.

Nani was a multi-faceted woman. She was strong and had endless energy; she welcomed panhandlers into her home to feed them and make them a fresh cup of coffee; she loved company and visiting with relatives in Tijuana; she attended daily Mass; and, she was a tough broad. Her language could be colorful – not colorful as in descriptive rhetoric, but colorful as in making a sailor blush. If she was mad, you got out of her way because, out of that gentle mouth, came a torrent of cuss words: from the mild *cabrón* and *pendejo* to the scandalous *tu madre, la puta que te parió* to the imaginative *shit con chile*. But that wasn't the end. When she finished with her Spanish litany of insults, she leaned forward and uttered the few good words she knew in English – *son of a bitchee!*

When I was in my early teens, Nani and I went to the local movie house, two blocks from home on Whittier Blvd. We sat at the end of an empty row and, at some point during the movie, a man sat at the opposite end of the row. As the movie progressed, the man inched his way closer to me and then began whispering to me. When Nani realized what was happening, she sat forward in her chair, looked at the man, and loudly unleashed a stream of the most colorful language in her repertoire. The man slithered out of the theater like a terrified reptile and Nani and I continued enjoying the movie.

Nani's only vice was smoking, assuming you don't include her illustrious cussing. She was a chain smoker of Lucky Strikes and apologized to no one for it. She was able to blow out perfectly round circles of smoke and was proud and happy to demonstrate her skill any time it was requested. A fondly remembered image is of her sitting outdoors under a shady spot, her stockings rolled down, wearing her sensible shoes, with coffee and a cigarette in her hands.

Cousin Pilar offers Hilda's story of how and when Nani took up smoking. During the Mexican Revolutionary War, Nani's brothers fought on the side of the *Federales* and would hide in the hills. Nani was possibly 12 or 13 at the time and her mother would send her with baskets of food for them. Hidden under the food was ammunition. Nani was understandably fearful and took up smoking as a way to calm herself. Her mother later took her to a Chinese doctor for help but he said to let her smoke since that was her way of coping with the stress.

Cousin Frank confesses he was intimately involved in Nani's smoking. When Nani lived with the Perea family and Frank was 8 or

16

9 years old, Nani would send him to the corner liquor store to buy her cigarettes (which they would happily sell to him). She would then take one out of the pack and ask him to light it for her on the stove burner (he swears he puffed but never inhaled). If he suggested that she not smoke, her reply was always the same, "Aww, shit!"

Growing up with extended family provided me more than good memories; it may have saved my emotional health. Mom was sick a good part of my early childhood and spent days in bed – sometimes hugging a hot water bottle to ease her *latido* (abdominal palpitations), other times probably depressed. For years, she couldn't walk a block or climb a flight of stairs without becoming overly-fatigued. She ate very little and, at first sight, doctors often assumed she had TB. Pops got me up and packed my school lunch in the morning, usually a toasted cheese sandwich.

When I was in the 4th grade, we had a school outing in the park and some mothers went with us. They joined the class in playing games on the grass and I was absolutely shocked. I didn't know mothers could throw a ball and run around – I simply had never seen that before. What I had seen was Mom reading in bed; devouring health reference books and enjoying magazines such as *McCalls* and *Ladies Home Journal*. I have never been a big reader and now I wonder if it wasn't because I associated reading with being sick.

There were times when I arrived home from school to a big pile of dirty dishes, probably including those of the night before. I felt like a complete martyr and remember having two fantasies as I scrubbed and toiled. One was that I would drop dead of pure exhaustion and as I lay on the floor dead, a tear would roll down my cheek and everybody would know I had been overworked and feel very, very sorry. The other was that Pops' parents would turn out to be rich and wonderful and, after searching for me all these years, would finally rescue me and I would live a life of luxury from then on. The dish washing routine may have only gone on for a couple of weeks when I was about eight, but in my memory, it was years and years. Actually, I have no clue whether it was weeks or years.

As the eldest in the family, Mom always held me responsible for what Sonia and Juan did or didn't do. When things went wrong, I either wasn't watching them correctly or I was setting a bad example. There were times when I was sure some mishap could not possibly be blamed on me, maybe I wasn't even around when the event occurred. But never fear, Mom would find the link and, sure enough, it was my fault. And, Mom wasn't above grabbing me by the arm and digging her long nails into my flesh.

Not all my childhood consisted of martyrdom. When I was in the 8th grade, I asked for a desk for Christmas so I could study in the bedroom. I had in mind an unassembled, unfinished item that Pops would put together and paint. Instead, I got a beautiful, solid maple desk that took center stage in the living room and was the best piece of furniture we owned. Then there was the fur cape Mom bought me to wear to the Junior Prom. We may have been poor but Mom had expensive taste and, every so often, she pulled it off. By the way, that old desk continues to serve me to this day.

III

COMING OF AGE

Lola had an infectious laugh – loud, hearty, genuine. It made you smile even though you had no idea what was so funny. She also had a beautiful singing voice and often broke into song, especially while doing house cleaning. I believe I was in the 8th grade when Lola entered the convent. Our family never travelled, so it was a very big deal when she left for St. Louis, Missouri. She was homesick and didn't stay long, however, maybe a few months. Upon her return, she told stories of witnessing segregation first hand. Her accounts of *White Only* and *Colored Only* signs on stores, restaurants and buses shocked us. We had heard and read about those things but had no idea they really existed. I think of Lola as the sensible one.

Hilda didn't take life too seriously. She was fun and flirtatious and loved spending time with her friends. She often included me which made me feel special and she was the one I went to if I had "boy" questions. When I was about 13, I was invited to a party. Mom let me go only because Hilda took me and promised to guard me like a dog. In retrospect, that couldn't have been much fun for her but she was gracious and acted as though she had a good time. She was an aunt, a big sister, and a second mom all rolled into one.

Ramiro was the mischievous one, a typical baby of the family who could get away with anything. He liked to joke and play and he teased me like a little sister. When he was 17, he talked Nani into letting him drop out of high school and join the army. He served in the Korean War and returned home when I was about 11. For a long time, he had nightmares and would wake up fighting and screaming. It was a hard time for everybody; PTSD was yet to be identified. Still, if I was running late for school in the morning, he would readily get up and drive me to the bus stop without complaint.

While I could go to Hilda to ask lightweight questions, there was no one to talk to about sex. The first time I asked Mom where babies came from, she said it was all in the Hail Mary. I repeated the prayer dozens of times but couldn't figure it out. Then, impatiently, she told me it was in the sentence that included "blessed is the fruit of thy womb, Jesus." Clear as mud but no further explanation. Then, in the 6th grade I told her that kids at school were talking about sex and something happening in the lower half of the body. She gave me "the look" and said, "You don't really want to know, do you?" Actually, by then I didn't.

As the years passed, I was too embarrassed to ask anyone and, with my friends, I just pretended that I knew. I found myself in high school without a clue what sex consisted of. Then, I had the brilliant idea to look it up in Mom's *Physical Culture* encyclopedia. Surely there would be a section on sex and reproduction. I snuck the volume that contained information starting with R and S out of Mom's bedroom and locked myself in the bathroom. However, once again, Mom was way ahead of me. The pages containing everything I ever wanted to know had been carefully torn out of the encyclopedia!

Since I had five kids and obviously figured it all out, I'll let you know that in high school a friend let me borrow a book her parents had given her many years before. She was a true friend – she didn't laugh.

20

When Hilda graduated from High School, I continued at OLQA but now the responsibility to get me to and from school rested entirely with Pops. I only remember that the commute became too difficult and Mom transferred me to another school in the middle of the fourth grade. I attended the newly built Santa Isabel School, about ½ mile walk from home, for the rest of the fourth grade and the first half of the fifth grade and then transferred again mid-year to St. Mary's School, near Hollenbeck Park and a one mile walk from home.

I don't remember why I transferred the second time since St. Mary's was so much further from home but that's where Mom wanted me. Fortunately, change has never been hard for me. Then, and all my life, I welcomed new schools, new neighborhoods, new job assignments, new experiences - anticipating the next one to be more exciting and rewarding than the previous one. So, after 2 ½ years at St. Mary's, I happily returned to OLQA in the eighth grade. I was eager to graduate from the same elementary school in which I started, especially since I planned to attend OLQA High School. All my friends from St. Mary's attended Bishop Conaty High School, a large girls' school with predominantly Anglo students. OLQA was a small school comprised largely of students of immigrant parents who spoke little English and had not graduated from high school (Pops went to school through the 9th grade and Mom the 11th grade).

I was completely comfortable at OLQA. All the students were just like me – except that they weren't. The parents of most of my classmates wanted their children to do well in school so they could get a good job. But one of my closest friends fought with her parents to stay in school. Her family's expectation was that children went to work at age 16 to help support the family. That was the reality of life. My mother, on the other hand, was fierce about education, not necessarily for pragmatic results but as an end in itself. She bought me my first dictionary at nine months of age. From first grade on, she supervised my homework and expected perfection. There was never any question that I was going to

21

college. I was always at the top of my class academically, but some of my classmates scored much higher than I on standardized tests. I knew they had greater basic intelligence but they had no incentive to perform. I, on the other hand, had no choice but to achieve.

Pops was always proud of me but he never pressured me in any way. Mom conducted the orchestra of my life while Pops stood quietly behind the curtain. If I needed help or permission for anything, I went to Mom. If I needed advice or just wanted to talk, I went to Mom. Pops did not engage in intellectual conversations or offer political or religious opinions. He was a concrete thinker who dealt with physical realities before him. He had a strong work ethic and financially supported his family. He was the ultimate build-it and fix-it guy around the house, from repairing the family car and all household appliances to building home additions. He did all the heavy household chores (mopping, vacuuming, scrubbing the toilet, etc.) because Mom was too weak to do anything strenuous. He provided transportation for the entire family since Nani and Mom never learned to drive. He carted me everywhere I had to go, often picking up several friends along the way – to school, church or the beach – never saying a word, never expecting anything in return. He was the one every member of the family depended on – and he came through like a rock.

Mom and Pops were not a typical Mexican couple, especially for their era. There was not one drop of macho blood in Pops and not one drop of subordinate blood in Mom. She was the thinker/decision-maker and he was the doer and that was fine with both of them. She worried and fussed about what could be and what might be while he savored the moment and took naps. He didn't blink an eye when Mom talked about her many suitors and how she could have married Chico or Ernesto – he was just happy he won the prize. I grew up thinking women should form their own opinions and that belief has served me well. I also grew up thinking women should be adored by their husbands and that didn't work out as well. My parents may not have been the most realistic role models, but their relationship worked for them.

Pops only worked at two companies while we lived on Mott Street: the U.S. Spring and Bumper Co. (primarily manufactured military parts) and Norris Thermador (primarily manufactured household appliances). When asked his occupation, he would put down forklift operator. He always worked the swing shift (approx. 4:00 p.m. - midnight) which allowed him to spend the day tending to the house, running errands, or driving one of us where we had to go. Every so often, he was laid off for several weeks at a time, and during those periods he did odd jobs around the neighborhood. There wasn't anything he couldn't fix and he was very dependable. Besides, the ladies loved him, much to Mom's displeasure. Mom allowed his handyman status only because it put food on the table while he was out of work.

The food on our table was always simple and pretty healthy. We ate meat when we could afford it but I do remember long stretches of time (perhaps when Pops was laid off) when we had beans for dinner every night – mashed beans, whole beans, beans with tortillas, beans with *birotes, tortilla mojada* – all delicious and a treat to look forward to. We never felt deprived and were certainly never undernourished. Mom was ahead of her time on issues of nutrition and exercise. She was a fan of Bernard McFadden (AKA Bernarr Macfadden) who promoted physical culture – a combination of body-building and nutrition. She treasured his *Encyclopedia of Physical Culture* and I'm sure read it from cover to cover. McFadden introduced her to healthy living and a distrust of the medical profession. Mom didn't believe in doctors, drugs, hormones, vaccines, sugar or fried food. She did believe in chiropractors, vitamins, enemas, whole wheat, honey, and beans.

By the time I was in high school, Mom had accumulated a vast knowledge of homeopathy, an alternative medical system based on the premise that "like cures like." Her interest began when she learned that British royalty embraced the practice, maintaining if it was good enough for Queen Elizabeth, it was good enough for her. She devoured William Boericke's *Homeopathic Materia Medica*, the bible of homeopathic remedies. She learned all she could from local homeopathic practitioners, who undoubtedly were charmed by her interest in the practice. She was a purist and looked for the one remedy that fit, not only the presenting symptom(s), but also the personality of the patient. Mom didn't like products designed for a particular ailment and consisting of multiple remedies. She later also developed a keen interest in Bach Flower Essences. I don't know the history of this interest but remember that she always had handy a vial of the *Rescue Remedy*. Mom became an excellent diagnostician and, until her death, ministered to the entire extended family. Most of us, to this day, continue the practice of homeopathy to some extent. But we all miss calling Mom and asking, "What should I take....?"

While Mom could eloquently expound on the merits of nutrition and exercise, she did not practice what she preached. She lectured me constantly; got me hooked on vitamin C when Linus Pauling proclaimed its many benefits and bought me a food grinder when it became popular to grind flax seeds. But nutrients and fresh vegetables hardly touched her lips. She loved her *pan dulce* (Mexican sweet bread) ignoring its white flour and sugar content. Mom maintained the same attitude toward exercise. She preached on the value of Jack Lanne's TV exercise program and watched it daily – from the comfort of her sofa.

I was 13 when my aunt Hilda got married; 14 when my aunt Lola got married; and almost 15 when my uncle Ramiro got married. This was fantasy time for a young teenager and I savored every minute of it. The dating, the engagements and the weddings were sheer excitement. Then the babies came. Before I turned 16, I had four baby cousins: Pilar, Ramon, Maria Elena, and Dodie (Dolores). I loved the babies and couldn't imagine anything nicer than holding and playing with them. I was in heaven!

Initially, Hilda and George lived just up the block and we saw them often. George's father owned a car repair shop (Ramos Bros. Garage) on the corner of Mott and Whittier Blvd. (across the street from Sanchez Market) and George and Hilda rented a little house right next to the shop. When they were first married, Lola and

Sotero lived between Soto and State streets, close to White Memorial Hospital. Later they moved to 85th street which was a distance away but it was a joy to see them when they visited. I don't remember seeing Ramiro and Gloria often, perhaps only on holidays and special occasions. When we got together in those early years, it was more than likely that Lola, Hilda and Gloria would be pregnant. By the time these prolific women were done, I had 20 cousins (and all within about 10 years!).

Seven weeks before my 16th birthday, a special bonus arrived: a baby brother named Francisco Jose but called Paco from the very beginning. Mom said that when he was born the doctor exclaimed, "This one's going to be a giant." In fact, when Paco was young and heard this story, he took it quite literally and was really scared – especially when he towered over all his classmates. Mom was obviously pleased to have had a baby at the same time as her younger siblings and everyone was happy.

Mom's theory of baby care was that the baby was never to be left alone. Paco was held continuously, even while asleep. Guess who did most of the holding? On the rare occasion that he slept on a bed, my job was to sit next to him, preferably patting or rubbing him on the back. Good thing he was a cuddly little guy. He was one of those babies that comfortably attached to your body so it was easy to hold, walk and dance with him. He was born in June and he and I spent the summer attached. Mom's timing was perfect.

The following summer (between my junior and senior years), I got a job at the same Sears store that Mom and Lola had worked in earlier. I was assigned to the cashier's cage (where Mom had worked) and learned to handle money quite adeptly. Jobs were easy to find back then and any teen who wanted to work, could. In fact, I hardly knew a 16-year-old who didn't have a job. I didn't drive, of course, and depended on public transportation and rides from family members. I wouldn't have been able to keep up my schedule had it not been for my uncle, Sotero's, generosity. I frequently worked till 10:00 pm and Mom didn't want me taking buses and streetcars that late at night. Pops didn't get home from his swing shift until much later. So, on those nights, Sotero picked me up at work and drove me home. It still blows me away to think that at least twice a week, this man who was probably watching TV with a baby or two on his lap, left his chair in order to pick up his teenage niece at work. Many years later, I thanked him and Lola for this and I honestly think they didn't remember what a thoughtful sacrifice they had made.

My high school years may have been the happiest and most carefree of my life. I loved school and every weekend could hardly wait for Monday to arrive. I was active in all school activities from the drama club to Our Lady's Sodality to journalism staff to thespian competitions – easy to do in a small school with a graduating class of around 60 students. In my senior year, I was Student Body President and, because we had a complete change of nuns that year, I took on more responsibility than I probably should have. I remember the young, new principal rolling her eyes as I walked into her office and sighing, "Now what, Madeline!"

I believe I was the only student in my high school who continued on to college immediately after graduation (although some went later and did quite well). Many students took shorthand and business classes and aspired to be private secretaries. I remember thinking that I didn't want to *be* a secretary; I wanted to *have* a secretary. I didn't exactly know what that would look like but I knew I'd recognize it when I saw it.

With a span of 4 ½ years between us, Sonia and I played together as children but didn't have a share-secrets or talk-about-boys relationship as teens. By the time I was in high school, I was so engrossed in my studies, school responsibilities, and friends that they took priority. I was happiest when I was outside the home and I didn't look back. That's too bad because true sister bonding did not happen between Sonia and me until after Mom died.

IV

THEN AND NOW

Growing up in the 40's and 50's was pretty uncomplicated. Here is a list of products and conveniences we take for granted today and how we managed when I was a child. It might have been different in other neighborhoods or parts of the country, but this was my reality.

Today, circa 2018   When I was a kid, circa 1950

Today, circa 2018	When I was a kid, circa 1950
Freeways	It took a long time to get places with no freeways, going probably 35-40 miles an hour. We didn't complain because we weren't in much of a hurry. The family looked forward to Sunday outings to the beach or the park, but often our outing simply consisted of "going for a ride" (that's where the expression "Sunday driver" comes from). Often, Pops drove us to the Pomona area which consisted of fruit orchards and open fields. I loved our Sunday drives, especially when we stopped for a root beer float along the way.

Turn Signals	We used hand signals; that's how I learned to drive – arm straight out for a left-hand turn, arm bent up for a right-hand turn and arm bent down to stop – no matter the weather or what you were wearing. Trucks had a mechanical arm that truckers could maneuver from the inside.
Seat Belts	Because there were no seat belts, you could squeeze a family of 10 into the family sedan. Babies sat on your lap, toddlers leaned against the driver in the front seat, children were stacked in the back seat, and all went flying when the driver stepped on the brakes. When you see people my age put their right arm out in front of a passenger when slowing down or stopping, it's because that became an automatic reflex.
Microwaves	We had a stove with an oven. The stove had long legs, a kind-of back splash with a ledge, and needed to be lit with a match. The oven was used for baking and for drying socks and small items. That was the only appliance in the house – no toaster, no blender, no mixer, no electric coffee maker. When Mom announced that she was going to bake, I knew I would be beating the batter 300 times by hand.
Dishwashers	In good times, I helped Mom wash or dry dishes. In bad times, I did it all myself. There were always dishes that needed to be washed in my house but Nani's kitchen was always clean. And, she never asked me to help her. I was 24 years old before I saw my first dishwasher at a friend's house.

Automatic Washer	I hated Saturdays because that was wash day. We had a wringer washing machine in the bathroom. The clothes would wash in the machine; then we'd manually rinse them in the bathtub and push each item through the wringer, taking great care to keep fingers, hair and sleeves from slipping through. Then we mopped the water off the floor.
Clothes Dryer	We had about five rows of clothes lines between our house and Nani's house and Nani had her own set of clothes lines behind her house. I started hanging clothes as soon as I could reach the lines. In high school, I starched my school uniform (jumper and blouse) so that, when dry, they could stand by themselves. Then, of course, everything had to be ironed.
Disposable Diapers	There were a lot of babies in the family and that meant a lot of cloth diapers. Diapers were rinsed in the toilet and kept in a diaper pail until they were washed, hung out to dry, and folded. When it rained, diapers were strewn throughout the house, on every possible surface, to dry.
Drive-Thru's	There were no drive-thru's of any kind – no drive-thru fast food, banks, pharmacies, or cleaners. There were a few Carls drive-ins, however, the kind where you parked and young attendants in skates hooked up a tray to the opened driver's side window and served you. Once George and Hilda took me with them to a Carls for a delightful treat and I also went to one after the Junior Prom. I think A&W Root Beer had a similar arrangement.

Convenience Food	Life was pretty predictable: fathers worked; mothers prepared three meals from scratch; and families sat down to eat together. I ran to the corner Sanchez Market daily (sometimes 2 or 3 times a day) to buy whatever we needed for the next meal. We did not have fast food on every corner, supermarket deli sections, frozen meals, or ready-to-eat packaged food.
Credit/Debit Cards	We paid for everything with cash. We did have an "account" at Sanchez Market and they kept track of what we spent in a small tablet. On payday, Pops would pay the bill. All bills were paid in person and the insurance man came to the house. I don't think my parents had a checking account until much later.
Computers	Everything was handwritten and penmanship was important. In high school, I took a typing class and had my own portable typewriter by the time I was a senior. In college, I wrote all my papers out in longhand and then typed my final copy. If I made a mistake, I often typed the entire page over again because erasing was such a mess. When "easy erase" paper came out, I was ecstatic and thought things couldn't get any better.
Copy Machines	We used carbon paper. It was messy and it got your fingers blue and purple but if you were careful, you could come out with a readable copy. Of course, it looked nothing like the original but no one seemed to mind.
Internet	Most middle-class households had a set of encyclopedias and that's what we used

	to do our research. If the encyclopedias were not enough, we went to the library. I felt like I lived at the County Library in downtown Los Angeles while in college. If we wanted to communicate with someone, we called them on the phone or wrote a letter. If the line was busy, we tried later. I remember when postcards were a penny to mail.
Cell Phones	Our first telephone was a "party line." This meant multiple households shared the same line and you could listen to other people's conversations if you were so inclined. Telephone operators were used extensively by businesses and were available to assist with any call problems, making this a popular occupation for girls right out of high school.
Flat TVs	We got our first television when I was about 10. It was a huge console with a little screen that showed black-and-white pictures. It was an electronic marvel and everybody wanted one. Soon, every house boasted an antenna on the roof. There were no remote controls so we got a lot of exercise, and no one thought anything of it. When the knob fell off, we used a skate key to turn the channel.
Organized Sports	We played spontaneously with kids in the neighborhood. I loved skating up and down the block although I never mastered a smooth stop. We also played jump rope and hopscotch on the sidewalk. Mom didn't encourage Sonia or me to participate in sports activities at school. I think she didn't consider it proper female behavior. I never had a bicycle growing up although I did learn to ride one (single speed with brakes at the feet, of

	course).
Video Games	My generation also had an array of games to be played inside the house. Girls entertained themselves for hours with paper dolls, jacks, and pick-up-sticks. We also wiled away the hours browsing through the Sears catalogue, especially that magical Christmas one. Boys played marbles and we all made tents and hiding places using chairs, blankets, sheets and a lot of imagination.
Designer Clothes	Sonia and I wore clothes designed by Mom when we were young. She was an excellent seamstress but, by the time I was in high school, we shopped the sales at Bullocks, The Broadway and May Co. in downtown L.A. Pops drove us to the stores early and when the doors opened the crowd raced for the good buys and if you were a few minutes late, all you saw were empty hangers swinging on the racks.
Eating Out	Eating out was a rare occasion. In fact, I can only remember two places where we had an occasional lunch - Cliftons, a lovely cafeteria where you could load your tray with all kinds of delectable goodies and Woolworth's where I always had the turkey club sandwich and a shake. Both were in downtown L.A. and we only ate there after a shopping spree.
911	If you had a telephone, you could dial the police or ambulance service directly, or get ahold of the operator. When my brother, Juan, was a toddler, he fell on top of an empty coffee can with a sharp edge and suffered a very deep cut. Mom ran screaming into the street

	and the mailman drove them to the local hospital. That's probably how most emergencies were handled.
Appearance	Women were just as concerned about their appearance back then; we just handled it differently. In high school, I weighed about 108 pounds but Mom made me wear a girdle when I dressed up – God forbid something might jiggle. We also wore full slips and never went bare-legged. Pants were strictly just for around the house or the park.
Wash 'n Wear Cuts	The washing and curling of hair was a pretty big deal. When I was little, we made our rollers out of 2" strips of shopping bag paper rolled over 6" strips of rags. We rolled the paper up a strand of hair and tied it with the strip of rag. My hair was long and I wore it in braids most of the time until I was 13. I remember sitting on the front porch with Nani combing my hair dry in the sun. When I was older, we curled our hair by rolling up a small strand with our fingers and securing it with a pin curl. There are actually videos online currently that demonstrate that procedure.
Daily Showers	I didn't live in a house with a shower until I got married. The first tub I remember was a *tina* (a large, round metal tub) that was placed in the kitchen and filled with water that had been heated on the stove. As a child in LA, I took a bath once a week or so but had a nightly routine of "washing up" for school.
Working Moms	It was highly unusual for mothers to work full time. If they did, it was a short-term job – not a career. Mom worked for short periods at the main Sears store off Soto as a

	cashier and later at our church rectory and school. I remember those periods as times when she was the happiest and the healthiest.
Instant Media	We got our news through newspapers and on newsreels between movies at the theater. Much later, we could see the news on major network television. Everything was well edited and objective. Personal opinions were seldom shared.
24/7	Most major stores were closed on Sunday (a day of rest) and nothing was open around-the-clock. People planned their shopping and errands ahead of time and the pace of life was pretty easy and steady.
Surgery	There were no imaging tests like CT Scans or MRIs so in order to learn what was wrong with you, doctors did major, exploratory surgery. Nothing minimally invasive, believe me.

V

COLLEGE & MARRIAGE

There was never any question I was going to college. That was my mother's plan from the day I was born. She had come so close to a university education herself but her father died unexpectedly before she finished high school and she had to work to help support the family. I think a little bit of her died when her life changed so abruptly, but her dream lived on in me and in my sister. Interestingly, this emphasis only applied to Sonia and me. Juan and Paco didn't have the same kind of pressure. I asked Mom about this many years later and she said they were men and men could always find a way to make it in the world, but women needed an education to ensure they would be all right.

I worked at Sears during my senior year of high school - full time in the summer and part-time during school. I applied for a California Merit scholarship but my SAT scores were not high enough. Nevertheless, when I started college, I had enough money saved to pay for my tuition, books and clothing. I remember standing in line to register and girls around me raising their eyebrows (in admiration) because I had cash in my hand. They had checks signed by their parents and really had no idea how hard I had worked for that money. In my college freshman year, I also worked at school in the Controller's Office. In my sophomore year, I was offered a full scholarship so I didn't have to work extra but I did continue at Sears for another year. It was really important to me that I not be a financial burden on my parents. It was a matter of pride, really, because they had always made sure my needs were met.

I knew I would be attending Immaculate Heart College – a small, liberal arts, Catholic college for women. It never occurred to me to apply anywhere else. Frankly, I would have gotten lost in a large university; I needed the family atmosphere of a small intellectual community. As it was, I went through a severe case of culture shock my freshman year. I was only one of a handful of Latina students in my class and was stunned when a classmate commented on my "thick" accent. And, for the first time in my life, I struggled academically. College was not fun for me and I did not take part in extracurricular activities. I lived at home and faced a long commute every day, often on public transportation. I didn't share the camaraderie associated with dorm or apartment living. I couldn't attend social and academic activities offered during late afternoon and evening hours. I was shy and reserved and hardly ever participated in class discussions (in sharp contrast to my high school experience). I studied non-stop and what I didn't understand I memorized. I longed for the day when a class or a book or a term paper didn't dictate the course of my day.

What saved me in college was that I could write. Sister Lenore (Dowling) had taught me English in the 8th grade and again in high school. She initially returned my writings covered in red ink for every grammar infraction or other imperfection with my prose. *Blah, blah* she would liberally write in the margin. I decided this was a challenge I was up to and I made it my goal to see less and less red ink on the pages I wrote. Eventually, I was down to a smidgen of red. I knew if I pleased Sr. Lenore, I was doing well and I was proud of it. In college, I counted on term papers to bring up my grade and they did.

I have always appreciated the role the Immaculate Heart Community played in my life. The IHM nuns were strong, forward-thinking, nurturing feminists. They required their elementary and high school teachers to be credentialed at a time when other religious orders didn't require a college degree. In fact, this was an ongoing bone of contention between the Immaculate Heart Order and Cardinal McIntyre of the Los Angeles Archdiocese who minimized the need for a college education. When I arrived at Immaculate Heart College, I was impressed by the number of IHM professors with a doctoral degree.

I was more impressed by the fact that the nuns expected students to think for themselves (demanded it, actually); no small thing for someone like myself who had been raised in a children-are-seen-and-not-heard environment and whose religion was authoritative and male-dominated. Every opinion, if logically articulated, was given credence and students were encouraged to explore every realm of possibility. We were respected and empowered to believe we could make a difference in the world as well as in the home. Women, at that time, were second-class citizens in the workplace but the IHMs made us believe we could do it all. I may not have recognized their effect until many years out of college, but the seeds they planted at that time germinated later when I needed them most.

I hadn't dated in high school and was still shy and awkward in college. I had been raised in an old-fashioned Mexican environment and Mom was overly protective. Not only did she not encourage social pursuits, she put the fear of God in me (although I had no idea what there was to fear). In high school, I had been involved in all kinds of activities, but none of them included boys. When I needed a date to a formal dance because I was an officer for the organization, Mom asked the mother of a boy I knew if he could take me. I was tense and guarded the whole evening and certainly not much fun. When I needed a date to the junior prom because, as junior class president, I had to pay the venue and the band, I asked a boy I knew from grammar school. I was the slightest bit more relaxed but still not much fun. I didn't attend my senior prom.

I told myself this was all part of a master plan. I would graduate from college, go on to graduate school, have a career, and then think about marriage, but certainly not before age 25 (any later than that and I would be considered an old maid). There was lots of time to think about boys and dating and I should be in no hurry.

Still, it was hard to listen to conversations about boyfriends and dating and not be able to join in. It was even harder to attend college mixers and not get asked to dance. There I stood, the classic wallflower, with a terrified *ask me/don't ask me* look on my face.

David and I met in March of my freshman year. I occasionally got together with high school friends and I invited two girlfriends to the Shakespearean play "As You Like It." One of the girls invited three boys as she had her eye on one of them. I wasn't happy with the arrangement because adding boys to the evening would just complicate it, but I couldn't get out of it. As it turned out, my friend was hoping to entice David. They belonged to the same parish and she knew his family.

I had a good time at the play. I learned David was 21 years old and had just come out of the Seminary, which he had entered before high school. He had intended to become a priest of the Claretian Order but had recently decided that was not his vocation. He was serious and articulate and I immediately said *yes* when he called a week later to ask me out. Over the next few months, we discovered we were pretty compatible – pseudo-intellectual (serious philosophy/theology discussions) and socially immature (absolutely no street smarts).

Our courtship was a formal one. David came to visit at an appointed time and we sat on the living room couch and talked – with Mom just around the corner. We went to dinner, school functions, and movies (if approved by the *Legion of Decency* – a Catholic classification of movies). We didn't hang out. We didn't even hold hands for six months.

I loved feeling "normal." I had a boyfriend; we went to school mixers and formal dances; I daydreamed during school lectures. My thoughts of grad school faded into the background and the fantasy of marriage and children took a more prominent position. I believed David and I were a perfect couple: serious, disciplined, religious, education-minded, seekers of the middle-class.

After dating for two years, David and I became engaged on Valentine's Day, 1961. I still had one year of college left and I promised Mom I would graduate – no matter what. David was also attending community college part-time, determined to get his BA at some point in the future. He worked full-time as a typist clerk for the LA County Road Department making about $320 a month.

We planned and paid for our own wedding. David bought our rings at *Gemco*, a membership department store, for $200. I bought my dress off the rack for $50 and borrowed a hoop skirt to wear underneath. We couldn't afford a photographer or musician but people took snapshots and a friend played the organ as a wedding gift. We both worked (I at a day camp) until 5:00 p.m. the day before the wedding. The ceremony took place at St. Anthony's Church in San Gabriel, with a priest friend of David's officiating. Pops roasted two turkeys and folks brought side dishes to our potluck reception at the house on Saxon Ave. that my family had moved into just weeks before. We drove to Santa Barbara for our honeymoon but didn't have advance reservations. There was some festival going on and we couldn't find a vacant motel so we backtracked and stayed a couple of nights in a motel in the Oxnard area.

I got married five days before my 21st birthday. That may be young by today's standards but not back then. An 18 year-old girl who had graduated from high school was considered of perfect marriageable age. Unmarried couples did not live together. They certainly did not have babies together. Nobody said it but young people often married so they could have sex. Things changed very quickly as the 60's progressed, but this was my world in the 50's and very early 60's.

The first apartment David and I rented was a $70 per month furnished studio on Normandie Avenue, about a mile from Immaculate Heart College. It had an "old" feel and smell to it but I was delighted I was able to walk to school. I loved being in love – with my husband, with my independence (from parents), with the idea of being a married college student. I was not sure the college would continue my scholarship because I was now married but they were surprised that I would even ask.

My marital status was more shocking to my classmates. Two of them came up to me and said they had seen me at the Loyola University library. They asked if I was there with my brother. I said I was there with my husband and their jaws dropped. They hadn't imagined I was there with a boyfriend, much less a husband. I think they had stereotyped me as a quiet, shy, socially inept person and that was that.

I was pregnant my entire senior year and became a mother a week before I graduated from college. Six years later, I had five children. Without much thought, I had happily traded in books and classes for diapers and runny noses. Gone were the lofty dreams of a career in psychology or law. I was elbow-deep in reality and I counted it as a good day when I could put one foot in front of the other. This all felt normal to me. I wanted a large family (certainly larger than five!) and easily transferred my dreams to my children. I pictured them at Notre Dame and then living in exotic places all over the world that I could visit.

Sadly, my big mistake was not being more like my own mother. I didn't push my children for academic excellence. I didn't push as though I had any expectations at all. Somehow I thought it would all just happen. I give Margaret abundant credit for pushing herself to an AA despite a learning disability. Vincent also pushed himself and in 2014 received a Doctorate in Ministry. Michael and Christopher were certainly smart enough but never got the support and encouragement they needed in their early years to pursue higher education. I blame myself for that. As the eldest, Michael was cheated out of childhood and Christopher suffered the most

40

when I went to work. Missed opportunities to read to your toddlers and make learning fun with your children turn into serious regrets once they're in high school. Given the chance, I would do that period in their lives over again.

My marriage did not turn out as I dreamed but I liked the idea of being married and I still believe in the institution. I don't know if there's a secret to a good marriage but I believe one important indicator is whether the parents of the bride and groom would be friends independent of the marriage (my mother and David's father hated one another). If the in-laws enjoy one another, it's likely they have similar values and philosophies and their offspring more apt to be compatible in important areas. I know couples who have been married over 50 years but they don't acknowledge any secrets. I envy that they have someone to grow old with; someone to know so well you finish their thoughts, could almost breathe for them. It just wasn't meant to be for me.

VI

BIRTH STORY - MICHAEL

Michael, you were born three days short of ten months after your dad and I got married. If I'd had my way, you would have been born one month earlier. I was desperate to get pregnant right away even though I still had one year left of college and I knew I had to graduate. Lots of babies were a natural thing in the family (Latinos and Catholic, what do you expect) and I had decided I wanted eight children so I guess I thought I'd better get going. As it turned out, you were due one week after graduation but arrived one week before. I attended the ceremony but could not participate so I heard myself graduate "in absentia." It sounded like I graduated with honors and I was happy indeed – a college graduate and a mother all at once!

Early in my pregnancy with you I started to threaten a miscarriage. The doctor gave me a prescription and I asked if it was a hormone. He acknowledged that it was and when I got home I tore the prescription up. Instead, I arranged for schoolmates to drive me to and from school and I restricted my activity as much as I could. I knew I wasn't going to lose you. As for the prescription, I'm now certain it was for DES, a synthetic estrogen that was later found

42

to cause serious health problems in people whose mothers took it during pregnancy.

When we learned that Kaiser was not going to cover the pregnancy and delivery because we hadn't been enrolled long enough, we had to make a plan for how to pay for you. At Mom's prompting, I went to a fancy OB-GYN on Wilshire Blvd. and he was expensive. So, just three months after moving into our studio apartment, we moved out. At that time, the front house on the property on Mott Street in Boyle Heights (where I grew up) was occupied by my aunt Lola, Sotero and their kids. My grandmother, Nani, lived in her one bedroom house at the back of the property. Without a second thought, Nani moved in with Lola's family so that your dad and I could use the back house and get ready for you. I'm still amazed at the sacrifice these folks made. Lola and Sotero had four small children and Lola was expecting her fifth (Carmen). Now Nani lived with them also – all in a tiny two-bedroom house.

It was not an easy pregnancy. I threw up constantly and felt wretched. At times, I did not have time to mop my breakfast off the floor before we had to rush to school. Your dad drove me to school, went to work and then picked me up in the evening. He also worked part-time at night for extra money – first in a bowling alley where he did custodial work, then in a hospital where he was assigned miscellaneous tasks. I did well in school and the nuns looked the other way when I was late to class or had to run out quickly. Actually, I was quite a spectacle and turned many heads: in the early 60's you didn't see many pregnant girls in an all-women Catholic college.

The week before you were born, I was completely preoccupied with final exams and term papers. I only had one paper left to complete when, on Saturday, June 2, I awoke with unusual fluttering in my stomach. I went to the doctor that morning and he had no idea that later that evening, he would be called out of a party to deliver you. We spent most of the day at Mom and Pops' house and Nani made me some tea (homegrown *Yerba Buena*) to calm my stomach. We did our usual weekend grocery shopping and went home.

By 9:00 p.m. we were pretty sure the fluttering in my stomach was not gas since it came in perfect timing. It hit me that this was it – the moment I had been preparing for and dreaming about. I had told the doctor I wanted natural childbirth and he had patted me on the head with a "we'll see." I had read books I found in the big public library in downtown L.A. on how women in Europe had given birth during World War II with bombs exploding around them. I had asked the doctor if your dad could be in the delivery room and he laughed. I was still determined to do it my way.

We got to Queen of Angels Hospital at 10:30 p.m. The nurse examined me and then called the doctor and told him to run. As I was being prepped for the delivery room, I thought, *wait, it's all going much too fast.* I wanted things to slow down so I could really enjoy the experience. In the delivery room, I told the doctor I wanted to watch so they positioned a mirror above me – a nice gesture but not too helpful. Then, at one minute before midnight, you were born. The doctor, who had been delivering babies for 20 years, kept telling me I did a wonderful job; most women in those days had epidurals and some were completely knocked out.

The doctor was surprised at how tiny you were. When they put you on the scale, I think the nurse blew on it to make sure it hit the four-pound mark. I told the doctor it was his fault for telling me not to gain too much weight. The doctor said your lungs were strong and you were perfectly healthy, but they quickly took you away and put you in an incubator. Things were different in those days. We could only see you through a glass wall – no touching of any kind. In fact, I didn't get to hold you until the day before you were discharged – two weeks or so after you were born.

They didn't let you go home until you weighed five pounds. The pediatrician cautioned us not to expose you to other children until you weighed 10 pounds, so I held you up for Lola and Sotero's kids to see you through a window. I don't remember how long it took you to double your weight, but it felt like forever. In the meantime, you and I were confined to the house. On July 4, your dad had the day off work and he and a friend (our best man) went off to play tennis. I was sitting on the bed holding you when they left and I was sitting on the bed holding you when they came back.

You were so fragile I was afraid to leave you for a minute. I would run to the clothes lines, hang a few diapers, run in to check on you, run back to hang more diapers, and so on. In fact, there were three steps on the front porch that I jumped every time – up and down, up and down. On a few occasions, I even asked Lola to stay with you while I went to the bathroom. To her credit, she never laughed at me or acted as though I wasn't making a perfectly natural request.

When you were six months old, we moved to a one-bedroom house on Marshall St. in San Gabriel, right behind St. Anthony's Church and two blocks from my parents. It was convenient to be able to walk to church, the market and my parents to do the wash. Mom told me early on that she was too young to be called grandma, so you and your siblings called them Mom and Pops just like I did.

You were an easy baby from the start. You ate often but you were pretty content between meals and not at all fussy. You loved being rocked in the cradle your dad made for you. When you were able to sit up, you stayed wherever I propped you and were never in a hurry to go anywhere. You didn't rush to crawl (about 10 months) or walk (14 months). Other than an ear infection at age 8 months, you were very healthy. I was determined to keep you that way and never let anything unhealthy cross your lips. I made your first birthday cake from scratch using all wholesome ingredients (no white flour or white sugar for you). I was furious when someone in the family offered you a cracker.

You were 16 months old when Vincent was born. You stayed with Mom and Pops while I was in the hospital and, when I came home, I made sure to greet you with a toy and without a baby so that you wouldn't be jealous. It didn't work. You were definitely not ready to share your life with a brother. You scratched my legs when I sat down to feed him. You opened drawers and scattered

45

the contents all over the floor when I was busy with him. And, you attempted to throw a basketball into the cradle to hit him. Once, I put you in the crib so I could sit and nurse Vincent (right next to you) and you were so upset you inched your way to the top of the railing and fell over on the floor. You cried with pain and anger, Vincent cried from the abrupt end to his feeding, and I cried with sheer frustration as I held the two of you. What a sight we must have been!

When Stephanie was born, you became the eldest of three children at exactly 2 ½ years of age. You were happy to have a baby sister although you quickly noticed that she was not developing like the other toddlers in the neighborhood. You said, "Mommy, the baby's broken – you need to take her back and get a new one." You didn't say it with malice. You were always gentle with her and helped me feed and comfort her. You were never embarrassed by her odd sounds or erratic behavior, nor did you apologize for her. "She has brain damage," you would calmly explain when your friends stared at her. You may not have understood what that meant, but in the ensuing years all the neighborhood kids came to accept her and be comfortable around her. You had set the pace.

When you were four, some of the neighborhood moms took their 4-year-olds to the local school for a summer pre-school program. On the first day, the other mothers hugged and kissed their kids goodbye. I shook your hand. I suddenly realized that since you were 2 ½ you had been my "big boy." You had not been treated as a baby for long and never enjoyed just being a toddler. Stephanie was an infant for years - she couldn't hold her head steady until she was eight months. There was always a baby to hold, to carry, to sing to – and it wasn't you because you were my "big boy." My expectations of you were totally unrealistic and unfair.

And, it didn't stop there. When you were exactly 4 ½ years old, Christopher was born and 20 months later, Margaret. You were then 6 years, 3 months old and the eldest of five children (one a perennial infant). You weren't my big boy anymore – you were my little man. Pretty much, you rose to the occasion. You were good-natured, helpful, undemanding. You enjoyed school and didn't mind showing your siblings the ropes. You were supportive when I went to work six months after Margaret was born, even though that meant a family of seven and a live-in Spanish-speaking babysitter crowded into a two-bedroom, one-bath home.

It's not unusual for parents to look back and wish they had done something differently as they raised their children. When I thought of you, I didn't wish I could go back and do it differently – I wished I could go back and have you all over again. Start fresh, from the beginning. I would hold you, carry you, sing to you, dance with you, read to you - often and for as long as you'd let me. I wish....

VII

BIRTH STORY - VINCENT

Vincent, I was really happy to be pregnant with you. I had wanted another baby right away and, despite the wretched morning sickness (more like all day, actually), the pregnancy was easy. I was excited when the contractions started in the early hours of the morning on October 23, 1963. I thought it best not to wake your father right away. He got up at about his usual time. I told him this was it and he calmly took his shower and got ready. We dropped off Michael at Mom and Pops' and headed to Kaiser Permanente Hospital on Sunset Ave. in Los Angeles. At the hospital, he walked me into the lobby, said goodbye, and went off to work.

We were grateful to have Kaiser and not have to pay out of pocket for the pregnancy or delivery. On the down side, Kaiser delivered babies in a mass production style. Pregnant women were not assigned an OB doctor but saw whoever was on duty on the days of their appointments. They didn't know which doctor, of the many they had seen, would deliver their baby – again, it was whoever was on duty when that time came. I hoped for an older doctor, one with lots of experience, confident and gentle. On my last regular appointment, I saw a young doctor with a baby face, hardly out of med school. *I don't want him*, I thought.

The labor room was large and impersonal. There were several beds and a curtain could be drawn around each bed to provide a minimum of privacy. Every so often, a nurse would pull open the curtain and ask how bad the pain was. Each time, I assured her I was all right and she would happily leave me alone. All around me, women were in various stages of whimpering to screaming. I soon realized that the only way to get any attention was to make a fuss and demand something for the pain. This posed a real dilemma for me because I knew how to handle the contractions and did not appear in distress, but I didn't want the nurses to forget I was there.

When I thought it was time, I got a nurse's attention and told her there was no rest between contractions. She hurried me to the delivery room. Finally, in walked the doctor and – yes, there he was – Dr. Baby Face. I told him I wanted natural childbirth and he looked very worried. He said he had never delivered a "natural" birth and I believed him because several times during the delivery, I had to reassure him that he was doing fine. The nurse propped me up so I could watch and at 10:20 a.m. you were born. You weighed 6 lbs. 5 oz. – small but yet the largest of all your siblings.

They wrapped you up and placed you in my arms as we were wheeled to my room. The nurse asked where my husband was; they couldn't find him in the waiting room with the rest of the dads. I told her that he was at work and she was livid. She wheeled us to a telephone and got him on the line. "Your wife has something to tell you," she said and she handed me the phone.

When they gave me the option of Rooming-In, I didn't hesitate to accept. This meant you could stay in my room rather than the nursery. It was a new concept and still rather awkward. There was a compartment next to the mom's bed that housed the baby. The baby could be seen through a glass panel and could be accessed by the mom through a sort-of large drawer. The baby could also be attended to by nursing staff who entered the compartment through their own door. In fact, they took over the feeding and changing during the night so the mom could sleep.

There were strict rules against anyone but the mom touching the baby. Visitors – including dads – could only see the baby through the glass panel. Once, your dad walked into the room when the nurse and I were attending you and the nurse asked him to wait outside. He was so angry (he said he was humiliated) that he left the hospital.

You were a pretty demanding baby from the start. Let's just say that you knew what you wanted and you wanted it now. There was no asking you to wait – whether it was to be fed, changed or be held. No pacifier, no leaving you in the crib to play. Fortunately for me, baby carriers were very popular at that time. I could sit you in the carrier and move you around so you were with me all the time. You were happy to watch me fold diapers, make dinner, etc. as long as we were communicating the whole time. Once, when you were eight months old, you woke up and wanted to eat. This meant at least three jars of baby food and I wasn't quite ready so I gave you a bottle to hold you for a few minutes. You took the (glass) bottle, stood up in your crib, looked at me defiantly, and with a dramatic swing threw the bottle on the floor, smashing it to pieces. You never took another bottle after that.

When you were just a few weeks old, your dad's father died. He was a longtime smoker and drinker and had been diagnosed with emphysema. His immediate cause of death was bronchitis. Your dad called me on the phone from the hospital. His voice cracked as he gave me the news but there were no further expressions of sorrow. We left you and Michael at Mom and Pops' to go to the funeral. When we returned 2-3 hours later to pick the two of you up, Mom told me she could not take care of more than one of you at a time. It was just physically impossible for her.

After your grandfather died, I never saw your grandmother Boom Boom (one of you called her that and it stuck) cry. I did see that she dressed up, put on lipstick and seemed to step more lightly. Your grandfather was an abusive man and she had been completely subject to him. She now wanted to be independent and find a job. One day, your dad drove her to downtown L.A. and dropped her off. Amazingly, before the end of the day she had been hired to work in the snack bar section of a department store. She worked in different sections of that store for many years. Initially, she alternated between living with us and with your dad's sister, and commuted to work using public transportation. She then shocked the family by marrying a man she hardly knew. Some family members doubted it, but I thought she was happy.

When you were just a few months old, your dad started attending Loyola University (before the merger with Marymount) full time during the day and working full time for the Sheriff's Department at night. He booked prisoners as they were brought to the L.A. County Jail. It was a grueling schedule for him and a difficult time for all of us. Some of the difficulty was created by the fact that I didn't drive. My mother never learned to drive and my aunts had learned later in life and only drove locally. Neither your dad nor I had ever given it much thought, especially since there was no money for a second car. Now, there was also no time to learn so I depended entirely on your dad to drive me to the grocery store and to doctor's appointments. Other than that and church on Sundays, we pretty much never went anyplace except an occasional visit at Mom and Pops'. In any spare time that I had, I helped your dad with his school work.

You know those strep throat infections you had so often, even as an adult? I've always felt guilty that I might have predisposed you to them. When you were an infant, I was so careful to make sure you were warm that I turned up the heat at night. Your cradle was about one foot away from the heater (the wall kind that you adjust manually). I'm sure you were much too warm and being that close to the heater couldn't have been good for you. Anyway, I didn't know any better at the time and I was so relieved when the strep throat roller coaster eased up a bit.

Our small bedroom had a full bed, a crib, and the cradle your dad had made. So, when I got pregnant with Stephanie we moved to a two-bedroom, one-bath house on Angeles St. in Rosemead. You and Michael had playmates there and were happy. Life was not easy, however. I was once again wretched with the pregnancy (every pregnancy).

You were a wiry, active, energetic baby and I thought you would walk early. At 7 months, you crawled expertly – no obstacle could get in your way. But you didn't walk until you were 17 months old. The doctor said you were fine and you would walk when you were ready. I think you were ready physically but not emotionally. You were 14 months old when Stephanie was born and you weren't ready to give up being a baby. You enjoyed being carried and attended to and having another infant in the family was not going to stop that.

You held no animosity toward Stephanie, however. You never acted as though she was taking me away from you. When I fed her, you were perfectly content to sit by me or stand next to me and put your head on my lap. Stephanie's care was so demanding and her development so slow that I'm sure there was considerable tension in the house. You didn't seem to mind the tension, though, as long as your needs were being met.

Thank God for the rocking horse! I don't remember where we got it or who gave it to us, nor do I remember exactly how old you were – maybe around 8 months. You loved the rocking horse and spent hours at a time going forward till the nose of the horse practically hit the floor and then all the way back, forward and back. I'm sure you don't really have a picture of it but people who saw you were horrified, sure you were going to fly off that thing. But, you never did – not once. Pleas from well-intentioned folks for us to tie you to the horse were not necessary. The two of you were as one.

When you were around four years of age, we enrolled you in a pre-school program - a couple of hours two or three days a week. On the first day, you clung to me and I had to stay with you the entire session. You were okay after that and your dad drove you to school and picked you up. One day, he was late getting to the school and you were not about to wait. You decided to walk home – at least two miles on the busy Francisquito Blvd. Your dad found you but not before the Sheriff's Department had been alerted and there were helicopters in the air looking for you.

Every time I look in my jewelry box, I see the "diamond" brooch you bought me at the Save-On Drug Store near the house. You loved giving gifts and never passed up an opportunity to buy me a present. I was really into potted plants in those days and lots of those plants started out as little $.49 gifts from you. I remember you asking for money for your birthday so you could buy Christmas presents two months later.

But, perhaps what I remember most about you was your ability to organize your days and your tasks. You went to the library and came home with stacks of books – not three days before an assignment was due like I would have done – but the very day the assignment was given. After school, you'd announce your schedule for the afternoon and evening: one hour of homework, two hours of baseball practice, dinner, one more hour of homework, one hour of television. And, you stuck to your schedule no matter what. You dazzled your fifth-grade teacher with 20 page school reports and practiced until you became a top batter in Little League.

From the beginning, you did things your way. You never procrastinated. You were methodical and persistent. You took the long view. Still, despite your successes, you were hard on yourself. Even as a toddler, you were always reaching for something that was just beyond your grasp. You tried to be perfect and then felt guilty if you did something perfectly. You imagined you were adopted. You didn't like being singled out or rewarded above your siblings. You were dramatic ("I don't think I'm going to make it," you said after your hernia surgery). Forget the rest, Vincent – you should always keep in mind one thing: you did good.

VIII

BIRTH STORY - STEPHANIE

Stephanie, you were born two minutes past midnight on December 30, 1964. Michael was exactly 2 ½ years of age and Vincent was 14 months old. The pregnancy was pretty uneventful except for the last week. The doctor told me you were not in a good position and I feared a breech birth. Mom took me to a *curandera* (folk healer) who manipulated you into a proper position and there was no problem with the delivery. You did have a hematoma on your head and looked a little like Gumby, but otherwise, everything proceeded as normal. I had heard that the third child was the easiest and I was ready for that. I was comfortable with the Kaiser system (had never met the doctor on duty who delivered you) and I happily asked for rooming-in since it had worked so well with Vincent. Above all, I was absolutely delighted to have a daughter!

I noticed right away there was something wrong, but I didn't know what the "something" was. I asked that the pediatrician doing rounds take a look at you – there was a vacant stare in your eyes and you had no interest in feeding. When he assured me that you were fine, I decided to relax and enjoy my baby girl.

When your dad arrived to visit, he brought flowers and a large stack of schoolbooks. I had been helping him write some term papers that were due at the end of the semester in January and he didn't want me to waste any time. Since I was determined not to "worry" about you, I focused on the paper-writing at the hospital and again when we got home. I was so happy that you were an easy baby, sleeping most of the day and sometimes even all night. I did notice a high-pitched cry that ended suddenly with you in a deep sleep but I refused to think there was something wrong – you were my third, easy baby and I was going to simply enjoy you.

When you were three weeks old, I could no longer rationalize your behavior. The high-pitched cry was now followed by a head-jerking and then a deep sleep. I called the pediatrician and he said to bring you in the following day. It was a Saturday and your dad had National Guard weekend duty so Pops drove us to Kaiser.

The doctor said you were probably having seizures and he needed to admit you for tests. We walked across the street to the hospital. I took your clothes off and the nurse said I could stay. I needed to hurry home because Mom was watching your brothers. I looked at you and didn't know what to do. The nurse undoubtedly thought it strange that a mother could so stoically leave her infant in the hospital. She didn't see the tears as I walked out of the hospital clutching your blanket and clothing. Pops and I were silent all the way home.

Seizures. I knew they could be caused by high fevers or B6 deficiencies. I also knew they were indicative of – and could further cause – brain damage. The doctor had said he would call me regularly to keep me informed and he kept his word. In fact, he called me daily. And, daily he told me there were no real answers. All the tests were negative. The seizures stopped with the administration of phenobarbital. You were otherwise healthy. After a week in the hospital, you were discharged with a "wait and see" prognosis.

Nothing is worse than the unknown. Life goes on day after day and everything that needs to get done gets done - and yet time stands still. You dare not think of the future because you have no idea what that will look like. At some point, the doctor did tell me

55

that you would probably never be normal but I lost sight of what "normal" was. You were my beautiful baby and my heart ached - day after day after day.

You were like a newborn infant for the first eight months of life. You couldn't hold your head up; you didn't kick off your blankets; you didn't gurgle or babble; you didn't try to roll over; you didn't reach for things; you didn't respond to baby-talk; you didn't look at me. You had occasional small seizures and your medication was adjusted accordingly. I took you to another pediatrician for a second opinion but he couldn't add anything positive to your prognosis.

When you were eight months old, you developed a fever and lost your appetite. I took you to the doctor (who by now was like an old friend) and he thought you had the flu. For the next week, I held your warm body and squirted formula into your mouth until, eventually, you would swallow it. I thought you were going to die.

In a moment of desperation, I asked Mom to find a *curandera* and my uncle, Sotero, drove us to see her. She said you had a *fontanela caida* – a fallen or sunken fontanel (soft spot on top of babies' heads). She performed a ritual which I cannot now remember but included some praying over you. Indeed, when she was done, the skin over your fontanel was no longer sunken. Right after that, a urine test confirmed you had a urinary tract infection and, with antibiotics, that crisis was over. You also had your last seizure at age eight months.

I look back at eight months as a turning point in your life. You finally started to develop, albeit ever so slowly. By the age of two you could sit up and eat solid food. Still, there was no mother's joy in watching you grow. You didn't coo and smile at friends or relatives; you didn't do "cute" things I could brag about; you didn't return my love. You did consume all my time and drain all my energy. And, you did scream.

The crying started when you were 18 months old. Tranquilizing medication made you stop eating and the doctor ran out of ideas. The cries became screams and soon you could easily scream 20 hours a day. Nothing consoled you. Holding and cuddling only made you scream even more as you stiffened your body in protest. When you were older, I sometimes put you on a blanket outdoors under a tree so that you could get some fresh air and a little sun as you screamed. I'm sure it looked cruel and I'm so grateful none of my neighbors or passersby reported me to child welfare.

Music – only music reached you and somehow subdued you. You spent hours on end lying next to that old Fisher stereo. We found a way to rig it so that the same album could play over and over again. The Beatles' *Rubber Soul*, Herb Alpert and the Tijuana Brass, Dionne Warwick – they were your favorites. They were my favorites, too, because they gave me snatches of peace as they entertained you and kept you still.

Christopher was born just before your second birthday. You would have thought that having another baby would have made it impossible to take care of you, but actually the opposite was true. Having a baby who was developing normally lightened the burden of caring for one that was not. A sense of normalcy re-entered the household.   It became easier to put your handicaps into perspective.

When you were two years old, I asked the pediatrician for a complete developmental examination at Children's Hospital in Los Angeles. You were evaluated by a developmental specialist, an ophthalmologist, an audiologist, a social worker and others. Their final diagnosis was "multiple-handicapped." You had some spasticity (the floppy variety), problems with vision, and severe retardation. Your hearing was excellent. They could find no evidence of a genetic problem. You did not suffer a birth injury. Whatever went wrong happened at the moment of conception.

When I got pregnant with Margaret, my two best friends worried that I wouldn't be able to handle you, a toddler (Christopher), and a baby. One of them told me about a hospital in the Pomona area that specialized in individuals with developmental disabilities. She thought they might be a good resource for us at this time. Mostly to pacify her, I contacted them and, to my surprise, they said I qualified as a "medical emergency." They agreed to admit you into the hospital for up to 90 days when I delivered your sister.

There were forms to fill out and interviews to attend. During a tour of the ward you would be in, I looked at the rows of cribs with babies and children – smelly, drooling, crying, staring, rocking, simply existing – and I thought, *no, my baby doesn't look like that; she isn't one of them.* I feared I had made a terrible mistake. Still, when Margaret was born, you went to the hospital – you had to. Your hospitalization brought needed relief for the family but you were not happy. You cried yourself hoarse and visiting you was such torture that, after just one month, we brought you home.

Thus began a long relationship with Pacific State Hospital (renamed Lanterman Developmental Center in 1979) whose independent diagnosis agreed completely with Children's Hospital. Upon discharge as an inpatient, you qualified for their Day Treatment Program. Thank God for federal funds that sustained programs in which you learned to walk, feed yourself, and use the potty. As hard as it was to get you to the hospital every day, it would have been impossible for me to give you what you needed on my own. That hospital, its programs, and its caring staff were our lifeline.

The first indication that you might need 24-hour care came when you were six and enrolled in a comprehensive potty training program. The social worker was compassionate as she explained that all the children in the program were making good progress except you – and you were the only one going home at night. You needed routine and order and it all broke down when you were out of the hospital. She convinced me to let you stay on a 24-hour basis until the potty training was completed. A few months later, you were trained and we were all happier.

Then came the inevitable discussion. Another social worker (equally compassionate) approached me with the idea that you might profit by placement in a six-bed group home supervised by

Continuing Care Services. She listened to my hysterical anger at the suggestion that someone else might be able to take better care of you. She persevered, painting a picture of what life must be for you, the frustrations you must face. You thrived on order and structure and those were the two things I couldn't give you. I consented to the placement.

Over the next six years, you lived in three different group homes but you remained very much a part of our lives. You came home every other weekend, Friday through Sunday, and for longer periods during holidays. When you changed homes, I arranged pre-placement visits to help with the transition and often played the role of social worker as well as mother. I bought your clothes, kept many of your medical appointments, and made sure your needs were taken care of. When the third group home announced that it was moving, I could not bear the thought of another residential and school change for you. I decided to bring you home.

Your siblings were older, very willing to help, and admirably compassionate. A bus took you every day to a local school that specialized in developmentally disabled children with oppositional behavior. When the doctor tried to wean you off your anti-seizure medication (after being seizure-free since eight months of age), you had one final – and grand mal – seizure while your father and Christopher were home with you. Your dad had never witnessed one of the dozens of seizures you had as an infant and this one took us completely by surprise. Needless to say, you were back on the medication immediately and to the present day.

You were home from age 12 to age 16. Your episodes of screaming continued – not constantly like before but still fiercely and without reason. At the dinner table, getting ready for school, at bath time, your screams and your, "No, I say no!" could jangle the calmest of nerves. Your behavior was unpredictable and unsocialized; it was impossible to take you on an outing. I could no longer pick you up and carry you off when you created a scene.

There were good moments too. It was gratifying to see how willing your siblings were to accommodate you and make you happy. There are good memories of Sonia's beach condo in Port Hueneme, of sitting on a blanket at the park watching fireworks, of the pizza parlor where normal loud noise muffled your sounds, and of going through McDonald's where you could mimic placing an order. When you were enjoying yourself the world knew it.

Music remained your primary love. You could tune your radio as expertly as any teenager, finding your favorite rock-n-roll and disco stations. And, amazingly, you could "sing" along with all the top hits. You have a lovely voice.

By age 16, you weighed more than I and you were remarkably strong. Frequently, your sister and I together had to forcibly dress you and when we were done we ached from your kicks, bites, blows and shoves. It was clear you could not live in a house full of teenagers with stereo and TV blasting or with a mother hovering and fretting and getting upset over you. It was clear you needed to be surrounded by people with whom you could do things and communicate – at your level, in your way. You didn't need the frustrations of living within a world that had no meaning for you.

I decided to make a life plan for you and began exploring residential facilities throughout Southern California. One alarmed me so much that I reported it to Community Care Licensing and it was subsequently closed down. I selected Salem Christian Homes in Ontario, CA but it had a long waiting list. I was not deterred. You went into respite care and five years later, at age 21, moved into the main Salem Christian Home facility. I had taken you for a pre-placement visit and talked to you about "Stephanie's new home" while you watched me pack your clothes. When we arrived, you walked in front of me, turned around, and said "Bye, Mommy." You knew you were home.

IX

BIRTH STORY - CHRISTOPHER

Christopher, I wanted your name to be special and gave it much more thought than I did when I named your siblings. I finally decided on Christopher in the hope you would have St. Christopher's brawn and Thomas in the hope you would have St. Thomas Aquinas' brain. I think I succeeded pretty well. But that didn't mean things were going to be easy for you, even at the beginning.

A couple of weeks before you were born, we were all sick. My main concern was Stephanie who was running a fever and vomiting. The pediatrician knew I wasn't feeling well and didn't want me out in the cold, so he sent a doctor to the house to see her (I still appreciate that kind gesture). The doctor said she had the stomach flu and I could hardly keep up with the dirty laundry, as my own symptoms got worse. A week before you were born I went to the hospital with stomach pains that I couldn't distinguish between the stomach flu and contractions. They said I was not in labor and I had the flu. "Hot tea and bed rest," they said. "Yeah," I said.

I was horribly sick the whole week before you were born – fierce stomach cramps with diarrhea and violent vomiting. As I retched uncontrollably, hovering over the toilet with Mom holding me from behind, I felt you doing summersaults, protesting the assault on your own little body. When I went to the hospital in labor, the nurse compared my weight with that taken just one week before. I had lost 12 pounds! I wondered how much weight you had lost and whether you were hurt by my illness.

You were born on December 16, 1966, at Kaiser Hospital in Bellflower, a new medical center. I had transferred from Kaiser Sunset to Bellflower when our wonderful pediatrician moved – he knew the family well and I wasn't about to lose him. At Bellflower, I was in a private labor room, a real luxury. The doctor ordered some cultures since I had obviously been very sick. The cultures came back positive for salmonella, a bacterial dysentery-type infection. The doctor was reassuring but said he would have to deliver you in the labor room. They couldn't chance contaminating the delivery room. There was also the possibility the infection could have been transferred to you.

Labor was the hardest with you, mostly because I was so tired of hurting and it was difficult to practice my self-taught natural childbirth. Actually, your birth was the most natural of all, with none of the amenities provided in the delivery room. The doctor and nurses improvised and you were born at 10 minutes before midnight – my third midnight baby. The doctor held you up, said "it's a boy" and whisked you off to be isolated. They didn't even weigh you for fear of contaminating the scale. I was given a strong sedative so I could finally sleep and I just briefly saw your dad who had been relegated to the waiting room along with the other expectant fathers.

When I awoke, I was in a private room but not the maternity ward. I don't know to this day where I was. I also didn't know where you were. I was ecstatic when the doctor came in and told me you were fine although, to be safe, they would be keeping you in isolation until you were discharged. I didn't get to see you until we went home two days later. In the meantime, I felt completely well and wasted no time in the hospital room. I did my Christmas cards and introduced you to the world with a little notation in the cards. It was good to be busy as I waited for the moment I could hold you in my arms.

Your dad and I had lots of dreams about how we were going to raise our family and, when I became pregnant with you, we knew it was time to buy a house. Your dad had graduated from college the previous year (June, 1965) and was now working as a social worker for the Department of Public Social Services. He was close to making his dream salary of $500 a month and the time was right.

We looked at some houses in the $12,000 - $17,000 range and then an ad caught my eye in the local paper. *Horse Property*, it said. We drove by to take a look and loved the rural feel of the area - no sidewalks and lots of horses and farm animals. The yard was huge by Los Angeles standards (90 X 150) with large Australian Mulberry trees surrounding the house and creating a canopy of shade that was breathtaking. We stood in the back yard and knew we had to have it. The house itself looked like a shack, ready to fall down. It didn't matter. This meant if we saved enough money we could tear it down and build our own house some day. We called the sellers. The property was on the market for $11,950.

The process was not easy. Banks refused a mortgage because the house was falling apart and had little value. So, your dad's brother found us a private lender for $7,000 and Mom and Pops helped us borrow the rest. Then we played the waiting game. We were waiting for you to be born and waiting for the house to close escrow and we didn't know which would come first.

Both happened on the same day – you were born and escrow closed. While you and I were in the hospital, your dad moved us to our new home. By "moved" I mean that he picked up furniture, packed boxes, clothes, dirty laundry, dishes, etc. from one house and put them in the other. He must have done it by himself because Mom and Pops were taking care of Stephanie. There was no one to unpack boxes, clean cupboards, or put anything in order – all of our belongings were strewn throughout the living room.

I was completely happy on the way home from the hospital. I felt good and you looked healthy. We bonded as I held you (no car seats or seat belts then) and I was thrilled to be going to our very own home. When we got to the house, Mom, Pops and your siblings were waiting for us. We walked into the house and I stood in the living room while your father put your cradle together. He and Mom then looked for the mattress and a blanket to put over it so that I could lay you down. Mom complained that she hadn't done any Christmas shopping, handed me Stephanie, told me not to do any sweeping or heavy lifting, and she and Pops left. I stood in the middle of the rubble, rolled up my sleeves, and went to work.

I should describe the house here, though I think you remember it. It was, maybe, 800 square feet. A large, Southern-style front porch led you into a long, narrow living/dining room. The rest of the rooms (two bedrooms, kitchen and bathroom) surrounded the living room and could only be accessed through that room. A tiny screened-in porch/laundry room was off the kitchen. Every surface was dilapidated; the floors were uneven; the bedrooms had no closets; and the vinyl floors and Formica counter tops were peeling. The icing on the cake was the electrical meter that hung in your bedroom (yes, the meter guy had to come in the house every month to read it).

On the day you came home, nothing mattered except that you were okay and we were in our own place. That doesn't mean getting things organized was easy. You needed well-deserved TLC, Stephanie was still an infant at not quite two years of age, Christmas was around the corner; and, did I mention, the plumbing wasn't working? I had to wash dishes and baby bottles in a dish pan in the bathtub for at least one week.

Still, the day after you came home, I had dinner on the table when your dad got home from work. Keep in mind that in those days there were no microwaves and few convenience foods. I don't know how I did it but by Christmas the house was in order; the Christmas tree was decorated; and there were presents under the tree. Thank God for the Sears catalogue. I ordered what I needed and your dad picked it up after work. Then I was up till the wee hours of the morning wrapping and decorating.

As luck would have it, we got more than presents for Christmas. Your brothers had caught colds while we were in the hospital and they only got sicker when we came home. I really tried to keep you away from them but at 10 days of age, you had your first cold. Fortunately, it wasn't a serious one but, a few days later, I was at the doctor's with 104-degree fever. Maybe I was more exhausted than anything. Your dad's mother came to stay with us for a week or two. She was a woman who understood adversity and that life had to go on. She was a huge help.

During the time we were all sick, a nurse from the Public Health Department came to investigate the cause of my salmonella. She asked a few questions and left very quickly. I think the sight of all of us in various stages of illness in that over-heated little house scared her off, poor woman.

Eventually, everyone was well and life settled into some semblance of normalcy. You were a good baby, very bright and curious. I loved holding you and singing to you. When you and I were alone in the house (Michael at school, Vincent at pre-school, Stephanie asleep), I was overwhelmed with the joy of you. You were responsive to my attention and gave back 200 percent. It was such delight to watch you grow and reach developmental milestones with ease. You were exactly what I needed when I was struggling with a screaming Stephanie. I know you don't believe it but you truly saved my emotional life.

I wish I could say I always protected your wellbeing. Like the time I gave you Stephanie's medication. I had a routine in which I propped Stephanie up and, with my finger, deftly thrust her meds from a spoon into her mouth. One day, when you were about six months old, you were propped up near her (probably in your high chair) and, like a robot, I thrust her meds from a spoon into *your* mouth. You swallowed immediately and I stared at you, unbelieving at first at what I had just done and then absolutely terrified. I called the pharmacist in a panic and he reassured me that you would be all right, in fact might sleep a little better than usual. He was right that you were okay but wrong that you would sleep better. Never again did I dispense medication in a robotic fashion – to anyone.

I did react purely from instinct one other time with you, however. You were about eight months old and had a cold; nothing out of the ordinary or concerning. Then in the middle of the night there it was – the sound of a barking seal alternating with a whistle coming out of you; nothing I had ever heard before. Without thinking twice, I ran with you to the bathroom and turned on the shower until we were both engulfed in steam. An eternity later (at least 20 minutes) you were sounding reasonably normal and I was breathing reasonably normally.

We were at the doctor's office the next morning and he diagnosed your cough as croup before he even walked in the room. He said it wasn't serious and you would be fine but he warned me the croupy cough could return and, if you turned blue, I should get you to the hospital. *If you turned blue?* Wait - if you turned blue, I should get you to a hospital a 30-minute drive away? The doctor read my mind and added that usually a car ride in the cool night air helps ease the cough – or, of course, we could do the shower routine again. Thankfully, you didn't turn blue. I would have seen it immediately because I didn't sleep a wink for the next 48 hours. You slumbered through while I sat next to your crib and watched every single breath you took. Of course, I would do that tonight again if I thought you were going to turn blue!

You were 20 months old when Margaret was born. You took it all in stride, never displaying any signs of jealousy. Nevertheless, there were times when I sat down to feed her and I could hear the glass milk bottles that were outside waiting for the milkman hitting against one another. You weren't trying to break them but you knew the sound would bring me running. Then you could look ever-so-innocent, even surprised by my presence. You had a knack for that, as your sixth-grade teacher described to me many years later – the ability to instigate some activity or problem without it ever looking like you were involved.

I went to work when you were two years old. Dr. Benjamin Spock, pediatric guru of the time, spoke out very strongly against mothers going to work when their children were two. Any other age was bad enough but not two, he said. I was caught in a damned-if-you-do, damned-if-you-don't dilemma. I could stay home until I didn't have any two-year-olds (who knows when that might be) and let our family economic situation continue to deteriorate or I could take a deep breath, say lots of prayers, and hope for the best. I decided on the latter. We'll never know how much damage that decision may have caused you. My heart still breaks when I remember the look on your face as the babysitter took you by the hand to walk you around the house and distract you while I left for work.

I'm comforted by the thought that your intellect didn't suffer as a result of my actions. Your kindergarten teacher couldn't believe how smart you were. She told me she was giving you a standardized test (one that was given individually to each student) and you were getting all the answers right. She got so excited over the prospect of having a student with a perfect score (it had never happened) that she felt she jinxed you and you missed the last question. She was very impressed with you and really loved having you in her class.

When your brothers had questions about the birds and the bees, they were happy to talk with your father. So, when you showed some interest in the topic of babies at about age seven, I asked you if you wanted to talk with your dad. "No," you said incredulously, "it happened to *you*." Yes, you went to the source and you wanted detailed and specific answers. I think I did okay on the physical aspects but I lost a little on the big picture. A short time after our talk, you were watching a documentary about a family with twelve children. You turned to me with eyes wide, "They did it twelve times!"

Maybe you grew up too fast. That's what happens when a kid is precocious and accepts more responsibility than should be given him. For example, you were more than Margaret's big brother – you were her protector. You taught her how to cross the street on the way to and from school. You threatened to beat up any bully who even considered bothering her. You told her where to kick any male stranger who approached her. If I didn't thank you then, I thank you now.

I have to say, your mysterious side kept me on my toes. There was a deep side to you and it was impossible to know what you were thinking. You often had a faraway look on your face; you were part of whatever activity was going on but also outside of whatever activity was going on. Were you thinking, plotting, imagining, dreaming, connecting with spirits? I don't know. What I do know is that you have an extraordinary memory; not just impressions of the past but vivid and poignant recollections way beyond normal. You also have dreams that precede reality in uncanny detail. I know nothing about the paranormal but I suspect that (whether or not you know it) you do.

You are the contemplative in the family – always musing, always creating, always with notebook or journal at the ready. Your notes, stories, poems and lyrics nourished and sustained you. And, they amazed the rest of us!

Chris, you were good company, even as a toddler. You enjoyed hanging out with me. But, best of all, you made me laugh......so many times, you made me laugh.

BIRTH STORY - MARGARET

Margaret, you were a turtle from the very beginning. When your high school basketball team members nicknamed you "Turtle" they were right on. During games, you used to slowly make your way to your favorite spot on the court and hang out there until someone threw you the ball. Then you would easily and calmly make your three-point basket. No scrambling for the ball – it was completely effortless. You even made the record book for most points scored in one game.

You should have been born on September 2nd right around midnight. I was pretty experienced with child bearing by the time you came around, so I knew. The nurse who was attending me knew too. We waited. The labor wasn't particularly bad. The nurse and I chatted pleasantly. You were just in no hurry to be born. You say now you were postponing your entry into the world to delay falling victim to your three older brothers. But I know better. You were just being a turtle. You were born at 2:45 a.m. on September 3, 1968 at Kaiser Bellflower.

My pregnancy with you had also been easy – kind of like an old friend. I desperately wanted you to be a girl but, of course, didn't say anything because I was going to love you either way. I had a sense of wellbeing and I knew you would be healthy. I even learned to drive while I was pregnant with you. I learned in a VW bus. Your dad showed me the basics and then I went through a driving school. I felt completely liberated when I got my driver's license. It was the beginning of a new era.

I enjoyed another form of liberation when I was pregnant with you. Nani, my grandmother, was furious that I didn't have a clothes dryer (this from a woman who washed her brothers' shirts in the river). She must have said something to your dad in her usual outspoken manner because he quickly bought us one. I can't describe the joy that appliance brought to my life. For six years, I had washed several loads of clothes and diapers daily and hung them out to dry, good weather or bad, healthy or sick. In the winter, my hands cracked and bled from the wet and cold. When it rained, clothes were strewn all over the house, a diaper on every surface.

Right after you were born the nurse asked if I wanted rooming-in. I believed in the concept of mother and infant togetherness (what could be more natural than that) but I said no. I hadn't realized how exhausted I was and I decided you might benefit more from a rested mom than an ever-present mom (though I felt mighty guilty). It turned out to be the right decision. They brought you to me several times during the day and I thoroughly enjoyed you while you were in my room. Then, they took you to the nursery and I was able to chill out. What a luxury to lie there with no responsibilities and even have my food brought to me.

The morning of the second day, I could hear the doctor making rounds and all the mothers asking if they could go home. When he got to me he told me I could go home that afternoon and I quietly said, "Do I *have* to?" He looked shocked but the nurse whispered in his ear that I had four little ones at home and gave him their ages. He nodded and smiled and said he thought I should stay one more day. I was embarrassed but relieved. Your dad wasn't relieved, though. He had arranged his work schedule around bringing us home that day. He was upset and said he wouldn't be able to pick us up the next day. So, I called Mom and Pops and they were there when we were discharged and drove us home.

When I went to the hospital to have you, Stephanie went to Pacific State Hospital for one month. I remember that as a good month – no illnesses, no traumas, just normal life. You were less than a week old when school started and I asked Mrs. Case from across the street to watch you so I could walk Michael (first grade) and Vincent (kindergarten) to school on their first day. She was nervous about it but agreed. After the first day, all the neighborhood kids walked the three blocks to Baldwin School and we parents never worried.

When we brought Stephanie home, the fun began. She was enrolled in the hospital's day program which meant I had to get her to and from the hospital every day. We had no choice but to adhere to a strict routine. By 9:00 a.m. I had all five of you dressed and fed and Michael and Vincent off to school. Then I put Stephanie and Christopher in the VW bus (I guess loose on the seat or the floor of the car since there were no car seats or seat belts) and laid you down in an infant car bed (they don't make them anymore since now all babies are strapped into infant seats). Fortunately, we could take Valley Blvd. into Pomona because I was a new driver and had not mastered the freeways. At about 4:00 p.m. we all piled into the bus again to pick Stephanie up. I remember it all going pretty smoothly. You were an easy baby and slept during both trips each day. I couldn't have done it if you had been a fussy or demanding baby. We continued this schedule until you were six months old and I went to work.

The decision to work did not come easily. Actually, your dad introduced the idea. He argued that we were never going to make it financially if I didn't work and I had a college degree going to waste. I argued that you and your siblings were too young to be left with a babysitter and my college degree would never go to waste. I couldn't begin to imagine delegating your care to someone else but I had to agree we would never build our dream home if we continued as we were. So I struck a deal with him. If he found someone willing to live in our home and take care of all of you, I would agree to work. Having to take you all out of your own home to a day care provider was a deal breaker.

I never thought he'd do it. Your dad found a woman who had recently arrived from Mexico; an undocumented immigrant needing to send money home to her own family. It wasn't great. She didn't speak or understand a word of English, but I kept my side of the bargain. The babysitter agreed to live in our two-bedroom, one-bath home, with five children, Monday through Friday, for $35 a week. I hesitated to tell Mom I was going to work for fear of her reaction but, unbelievably, she was absolutely delighted.

At that time, the Department of Public Social Services hired social workers almost continuously and, in no time at all, I had a job. For the first year or so, I got about four hours of sleep a night – to bed at about 2:00 a.m., up at about 6:00 a.m. (keep in mind I had three of you in diapers). I had Stephanie dressed, fed and ready to go by about 7:00 a.m. so your dad could drive her to the hospital before he went to work. Then I got the rest of you ready. When you were all older, the babysitter helped with dressing and breakfast but initially I made it my job. After work, I picked Stephanie up at the hospital on the way home.

I worked in West Covina, just a 12-minute drive from home, so I didn't have to leave until 8:15 a.m. I liked being able to spend a little quality time with you before rushing off. Whenever I could, I arranged my schedule so I could come home for lunch to hold and feed you. I was really fortunate to have a flexible job in which I could pop in and check on you whenever I was in the area. And, no matter what time I dropped by, you looked content.

The fact you were contented had nothing to do with the babysitter because, actually, you must have had a dozen babysitters over the years. Many were Spanish-speaking, some were young, some quite old, one was pregnant, one quit after one week, two were fired, one seduced the contractor building our house, one was your cousin, and from time to time Boom Boom stayed with us. You were simply a contented baby and all the babysitters enjoyed you.

By far you were the happiest baby and child I've ever known. Happy when you woke up; happy as you fell asleep; happy to watch whatever was going on from your crib in the living room; happy to learn tap and ballet at the YWCA; happy to be the first girl in your farm Little League. You were even happy when I read you bedtime stories and inevitably fell asleep (me, not you). Your good nature continued as you got older and I don't remember having to discipline you. The only time I ever got upset with you was when you stayed home from Junior High after missing the school bus (you made up for it by having perfect attendance your four years of high school). You were self-confident, cooperative, and agreeable at home and at school. In fact, your academic needs were missed by most teachers because all they saw was a "delightful" child in their classrooms.

When you were 15 months old, you were walking pretty well except that you were still hanging on to whatever was around you. You were hesitant to let go and walk unassisted. One evening, I got home from work with Stephanie and made an announcement. Just a half hour earlier, she had walked to me for the first time when I arrived at the hospital to pick her up. As Stephanie showed off her new skill amidst clapping and lots of "good girl" praises from the family, you decided you wanted some of that joyful affirmation for yourself. So without a second thought, you joined Stephanie and neither of you ever held on to anything again. On the same day in December of 1969, you and your sister took your first unassisted steps.

When I went to work, my entire $641 salary went into savings for our new house. My splurge money was my $15 bilingual bonus and my mileage compensation. Eighteen months later, right after your second birthday, we were ready to begin new construction. We moved temporarily into a small house just a couple of blocks away – across from K&C Market, the little mom & pop store we frequented. I had found a drawing of a perfect house in a magazine and sent away for the plans. We made minor adjustments and an architect friend of your dad's prepared the blueprint. We went back to the private lender who had helped us buy the original house and we borrowed $20,000 for our new house.

Your dad hired a contractor/builder and they demolished the old house by themselves. Believe me, it didn't take much; it was ready to come down. Into a large trash bin the house pieces went and off to the dump. Your brothers enjoyed playing in the debris but you were too young to join them. Your dad worked alongside the builder on the foundation and framing and specialty work was subcontracted as necessary. I don't remember doing much – your dad made all the decisions regarding cabinets, countertops, and fixtures. We moved in around April, 1971.

In the end, ours was by far the best house on the block. It was Mediterranean in style with a stucco exterior, Spanish-tile roof, Mexican pavers leading up to rustic dark wood double-doors, and exposed beams throughout the interior. It had four bedrooms, 2 ½ baths, a family room, formal dining room, and laundry area next to the kitchen. It also had typical 70's features: split-level (two steps down to the living and family rooms), a floor to ceiling stone fireplace with no mantel, and dark paneling in the living and dining rooms and in the master bedroom. And, of course, there was the wall-to-wall avocado green shag carpeting, avocado-colored appliances, lots of ceramic tile, and linoleum floors in kitchen and bathrooms. You lived in this house from age two until you moved out. Then you returned to camp out in it while it was being sold.

When you were in kindergarten, your class put on a song for the annual Christmas Show. You were on stage with 30 or so other children, all looking for their parents in the audience and waving franticly when they spotted them. You were looking around, thoroughly enjoying yourself, singing your heart out and dancing to the tune. In fact, you were the only one on stage dancing at all since that wasn't part of the program. I realized then as I have many, many times since that you march to your own drummer – easily, confidently, thoughtfully, with strong convictions. I've always admired you for that and, yes, even envied you.

74

XI

BROTHER JUAN
NEPHEW JUAN

I was eight when my brother, Juan, was born. I remember him as a baby and toddler but, I must confess, I have trouble remembering him any older than about age five. He was almost 13 when I got married and memories of him are hazy. The snapshots in my head are just a little sharper from about age 17 until he died at age 21 – obstinate teenager, fishing in the Channel Islands, judo expert, entry into the Air Force, early marriage....

On March 18, 1970, the phone rang at about 5:00 am and it was Mom telling me that Juan had been seriously injured in an accidental shooting and was undergoing surgery. I cried a bit but comforted myself with the thought that this might result in his being discharged from the Air Force. It would be nice to have him and his new bride home. I went back to sleep.

Mom called back a couple of hours later to tell me Juan had died on the operating table. I rushed to Mom and Pops' house without saying a word to the kids. I didn't know what to tell them because I didn't know what had happened. This had to be a terrible mistake, I told myself. Juan was only 21 years old and had his whole life ahead of him. In fact, he had just called Mom a few days before to let her know she was going to be a grandmother. He and my parents and siblings had kept in close touch since he joined the Air Force. He was happy; he was healthy. Happy, healthy little brothers don't just die!

When I reached the house, Pops met me at the door and I knew there was no mistake. I had never seen Pops cry and he wasn't crying now – but his face was ashen and contorted with anguish, a look I'll never forget. I overheard him call his boss to report that he was going to miss work because his son had died and my heart broke for him. Mom, however, was surprisingly calm, comforting family members and friends who were arriving at the house, all looking like zombies.

These were the same people who just two months earlier had attended a joyful wedding – Juan's marriage to Kimberly. Juan met Kim while stationed at Tacoma Air Force Base in Washington, his first serious girlfriend. Their decision to get married in Los Angeles was an easy one – Kim's family in Washington consisted of her parents and a sister but Juan's family in LA was huge. And so on January 17, 1970, St. Anthony's Church in San Gabriel was packed as Juan and Kim became husband and wife.

Now there was a funeral to arrange. When death comes unexpectedly, there is no script to follow. Your world has changed from one minute to the next and it is no longer within your control. You want it to stop so you can begin to wrap your mind around what's happening, but you find yourself simply reacting like a robot to the need in front of you. People have to eat; the phone has to be answered; funeral decisions have to be made. I went with Pops to the mortuary but we didn't know what information to take with us. What do you mean you can't do anything without Juan's Social Security number!

Then there was the trip to LAX to meet the body. You are surrounded by hundreds of people – mostly happy, many tired, some rushed. They don't see the weight of pain you carry as you drag your feet toward the gate. We pressed against the window as we watched the casket being unloaded from the plane onto the hearse. We were also all watching Mom, expecting her to break down at any moment. Amazingly, she didn't. She and Kim were completely composed as we left the airport and, in fact, throughout the funeral ordeal. It was as though each was setting the pace for the other. This was the strongest I had ever seen Mom and the strongest she would ever be.

In January, St. Anthony's Church had been the scene of a celebratory wedding. Two months later, the same church was the scene of a heart-wrenching funeral. I looked around – it was the same people, of course. For some reason, my eye fell on a friend of Juan's – older, married, with children, a big guy. During the wedding, he had had a bigger-than-life grin on his face. Now he was sobbing inconsolably. The Mass and burial are but a blur to me now, but I am in tears again as I relive the fading memories.

The circumstances of Juan's death were unfolding even as we were burying him. According to an Air Force investigation, Juan tripped in his home while cleaning his rifle and accidentally shot himself. The bullet penetrated his liver and, essentially, he bled out. The letter from Air Force officials was terse; there was no formal investigative report sent to the family. I don't remember questioning anything or asking for further details. The larger story took shape over time as Mom talked with Kim and as we all tried to make sense of the accident.

This is the account I remember. Kim worked as a hairdresser and Juan planned to pick her up from work when she got out at 10:00 pm. He decided to clean his rifle while he waited and had everything he needed neatly laid out on a table. Juan had prior experience with rifles and was meticulous in their care and maintenance. However, it appears that when he emptied the rifle, one round remained in the chamber. Somehow he tripped on a throw rug while carrying the rifle and it discharged, the bullet entering his body. Juan was able to leave the house in an attempt to rouse someone and neighbors called the police when they heard strange noises. He lost consciousness right after alerting the police that his wife needed to be picked up from work. He was rushed to the hospital and died from loss of blood.

My siblings and I may have slightly different memories of that account. What we have in common are gnawing questions that have been eating away at us all these many years. If Juan was able to get out of the house, why didn't he pick up the phone to get help? Didn't anyone hear the gunshot? How is the shooting as described logistically possible? Was he distracted? What did Mom say to him when he announced to her that Kim had become pregnant before the wedding? (She had been very disappointed and chastised him for the bad example he set for the many younger cousins in the family.) Was he feeling guilty? Did he subconsciously allow (not cause) the accident to happen? We'll probably go to our own deaths never getting close to knowing the answers, but that doesn't keep us from speculating and from anguishing.

There's always lots of guilt to go around after a death. I don't remember when I told my kids that Juan had died but it was well after the funeral. Michael, the oldest, was eight at the time and was Juan's godson. He was fond of his godfather and certainly old enough to understand the concept of death. Margaret, the youngest, was 18 months and would not understand anything. I told myself they were all too young and the wake and funeral would be hard for them. But the likely answer is that it would have been hard for me. I didn't want one more responsibility on my plate, one more thing to think about, one more issue to deal with - so I rationalized it away. The kids' daily routine was not interrupted and I put on a happy face when I came home at night. Maybe that's just how people cope.

A more legitimate reason for guilt is how we all allowed Paco/Frank to get lost in the mourning process. Mom and Pops had each other to cling to, Kim had a wide circle of sympathy and support, Sonia had a new husband and a very strong bond with Mom, and I had my own family to tend to. Frank, age 13, had no one. Had he been younger, we might have been more attuned to what he was thinking and feeling; had he been older, he might have been able to articulate his thoughts and feelings for himself. But instead, he was left on his own to make sense of a terrible tragedy. Behind that bewildered face must have been such isolation. I'm so sorry, Frank!

I don't remember whether I took more time off than the three days of bereavement leave allowed by the County. When I returned to work there was a plant with a nice card from my co-workers on my desk. I got the requisite hugs and condolences. But no one looked at me. No one asked how I felt. I knew they were either trying to be respectful or felt awkward broaching the subject. But I needed to talk. Finally, I grabbed my desk mate and begged, "Let me tell you how awful it was!" Since then, I've learned to leave a little opening for those in mourning. Something simple like, "It must have been awful..." They are usually anxious to talk – because it always is.

After my brother's death, his wife moved to Los Angeles County and their son, Juan d'Amato, was born on August 7, 1970. He was a wiry baby and a hyperactive child with disarming charm and learning disabilities. Mom adored him and was often at odds with his mother about one issue or another related to Juan. His teenage years were troubled and included leaving home, experimenting with drugs and alcohol, and a diagnosis of paranoid schizophrenia. He spent his adult life at Metropolitan State Hospital and mental health halfway houses. I was his conservator for five years until I moved north. My sister was his persevering guardian angel. Juan died in 2006 at the age of 36. His death certificate lists the cause of death as alcoholism.

You may wonder why I've devoted so little space to the details of nephew Juan's life. The truth is I was only tangentially involved with Juan as he was growing up and my memories of him are mostly drawn from family conversations over the years. What I know without a doubt is that he was loved by his immediate and extended family, even though at times that love resulted in his being torn between his mother and his grandmother. Yes, there were mistakes made on all sides, but in the end, his mental health issues overwhelmed everyone and depleted their energies. The tragedy of Juan's life began before he was born and never let up. My sister and I learned of his death while we were vacationing in Budapest via an email. There was nothing left for us to do but celebrate a quiet Mass when we returned home.

XII

THE VIOLENCE

Things are not always as they appear. It would be helpful if domestic batterers, child molesters, and serial killers looked like monsters – maybe had an extra eye in the middle of their foreheads or were otherwise frightening looking. But often the opposite is true. They can easily look like the hard-working guy in the next cubicle at work or the man sitting in the church pew in front of you holding his infant son. They can be the president of your service club, the pillar of the community, the guy you trust in your home and with your children. They come across as personable and engaging and charming – yes, especially charming. But only they and their victims know what might lurk behind this attractive and disarming exterior.

Everyone thought he adored me. When we were together (especially at job-related functions) he was attentive and solicitous. He looked at me lovingly and treated me like a china doll. On the way to the function, he may have berated me for that pimple on my neck that was surely a sign of poor hygiene (and maybe I did it on purpose to spoil the event). But once we were there, he smiled broadly and had eyes only for me. He bragged about me and blended truth with lies. The truth: I had briefly taken piano lessons as a child. The lie: I was an accomplished pianist. People sometimes commented on things having to do with me or my family and I had absolutely no idea what they were talking about.

It was important for David to look good, to do well, to be liked and respected. And since I was an extension of him, it was equally important for me to be the perfect wife – or should I say, the perfect accessory. That's really what I was, an accessory to be used or not depending on the occasion. If the function was one in which he needed to mingle freely and negotiate, then he left me at home. If the function was one in which he profited by having a devoted wife by his side, then I was there.

I can't look back and say there were no signs. Yes, they were there from the beginning. Some were subtle and fleeting, like the time Pops called him "boy." David's face turned red and the veins in his temple bulged and he left my house in a hurry. He called on the phone to apologize and I quickly dismissed the whole incident as insignificant.

Some signs were not subtle at all. When we were engaged, I wore my engagement ring on my left hand and my college ring on my right. One day, David took my hands in his and suggested gently that I should pursue the college ring and abandon the other. I couldn't imagine what he was talking about. Then he promised that he would never hit me. I stifled a laugh and thought, *What a silly thing to say – why would anyone want to hit me!* I knew his father had beaten his mother, but what did that have to do with us? I was young and naïve and in love. There was no way I could have dreamed that the soft-spoken man I was engaged to could turn into his abusive father.

It's hard to know when it started. People always ask, "Why didn't she leave the first time he raised his hand to her?" Women often say, "If it was me, I would have left the first time he threatened me." But when is the first time? Is it when he throws a dish towel at you (how does that sound – "I left because he threw a dish towel at me!")? Or is it when he gives you a bit of a shove – hardly anything that anyone else would notice? Maybe the first time he grabs both your arms and squeezes them hard? But he was so sorry after and so sweet. Always sorry…always sweet. After a while it becomes a familiar pattern and you find yourself looking forward to the sweet.

If it all started with a trip to the ER with black eyes and a broken nose it would be easy. You'd simply leave and everyone around you would support you. But it's all much more insidious than that. You don't even know it's abuse - you think it's life, your cross to bear, a tough time - your fault, maybe, for getting married too young, for not having street smarts, for not developing better domestic skills. David and I were married for 17 years and, with perfect hindsight now, I understand the progression from growing up in a violent environment to creating a violent environment. But when you're in the middle of it, you don't see the big picture. And, you certainly don't see the emotional piece.

The emotional stuff is hard to describe. It's always there, chipping away at your self-esteem until you have no sense of who you really are. Your hair is stringy, you smell, you can't cook, you don't do things for the house that other wives do, you can't……you don't……you never……all uttered with such disgust and contempt. But there wasn't just me to criticize – there was my entire family. Over the years, my parents, siblings, even extended family were subject to the cruelest comments and deprecating remarks, albeit for my ears only. Finally, David stopped going to my parents' home or attending family functions altogether.

If there was one period of time that stands out as a particularly difficult one, it was when we were building our new home. We rented a small house a couple of blocks away while we demolished the old shack and built our dream home. These are stressful times, as anyone who has lived through new construction or renovation well knows. David worked side-by-side with the contractor, kept up a demanding job, and took his frustrations out on me.

One evening, I prepared the five kids for their nightly bath. Michael, the oldest, was eight and Margaret, the youngest, was two. I generally bathed two or three of them at a time so it was pretty hectic. David came to the door of the bathroom and told me not to have all the kids in the bathroom at the same time (probably to curb the noise). I told him we were fine – that I always did it this way. He told me again. I was so focused on what I was doing that I didn't pick up the cues. In a sudden rage, he shoved me into the bathtub (with a couple of kids) and held my head under the water. I don't remember that he said a word; I only remember thinking that my children were watching this. It was just a few seconds but all the kids were hysterical. I quickly wrapped a towel around my head to contain my wet hair and continued the baths while attempting to soothe the kids and reassure them that everything was fine.

The six months that it took to build the house were rough. It was during this time that David told me that he prayed I would crash on the freeway and be killed. He said it with such a look of loathing that I knew he meant it. I was a social worker who spent part of every day making home calls and I cried as I traveled the freeways of LA, wearing sunglasses when I talked with clients and telling them I had a cold.

It was also during this time that David first placed a pillow over my face at night. I quickly learned there was no point in struggling – he was much stronger than I was. All I could do was pretend to pass out. I didn't fool him, of course, but I also didn't think he really meant to kill me in such an obvious manner. That wasn't his style.

I thought surely the marriage was over – and the prospect both relieved and terrified me. David was unable to control his rage and I think even he started to recognize it. For a couple of weeks, he stayed in a small trailer parked behind the new house. He talked about just wanting to finish the home (for his kids) before he left. When he was sick with a cold and his romantic interest came to the rented house while I was at work to bring him cold medication, I thought we had come to a natural end.

But the cycle of violence isn't that easy to break. That's because it isn't just one thing – it's many things. In our case, it was his public image as a good husband, father, and provider (how could he let co-workers and neighbors know he failed); his genuine desire to be better than his father (he knew the truth deep inside him); his need to control me (if he picked me, I better be good); my need to maintain the secret (I never shared what was going on with family or friends); my image of myself (I have to keep the family intact at all cost); my religious convictions (this was my cross to bear); and the ever-present rationalization (this is only hurting me, not my kids).

And so, nothing changed. We moved into our beautiful new house and were distracted by everything that needed to be done. David did question my every move; where I was going, who I was putting on lipstick or getting dressed up for – sure I was having an affair with every man I encountered. But I got into the habit of taking Margaret with me everywhere I went evenings and weekends and that helped. Overall, things seemed better. Work was good for both of us and we turned a financial corner. We were enjoying middle-class and, to all outward appearances, we were happy.

But the dark side hadn't gone away. People handle anger in different ways: some lash out immediately, some keep it inside, some vent it appropriately, some punish an identified scapegoat. The way David reacted to stress and anger became more apparent after we moved into our new home. When stressed or angry, he didn't lash out immediately but neither did he keep it inside. For years, he demonstrated what I call escalating rage.

It started with the slightest trigger – some incident at work, getting home from work hungry, my facial expression, boisterous kids, the weather, a misplaced TV remote, almost anything. He might not say anything initially but we all recognized the look – the tightness in his face and bulging veins at the temple. The look got worse and his remarks more caustic with every passing hour. The tension in the air was suffocating and the kids stayed out of his way. I knew what was coming next.

When the kids were asleep and the bedroom door was locked, he unleashed his anger by attacking me sexually. This wasn't love – this was cold, hard, vindictive sex. This was rape. Sometimes I fought back, sometimes I cried, sometimes I went limp.

Always I felt trapped and completely helpless. If I screamed, I would wake the kids and simply bring them into the fray (much better that they not know what was going on).

Most nights I delayed going to bed and, when David was asleep, I'd crawl into bed just as softly as I could, holding my breath. I lay on the edge of the bed, my entire body in controlled tension, praying he didn't awaken. Most of the time, he did. Sometimes, I took a chance and lay down on the sofa or on Stephanie's empty bed but, inevitably, he would awaken during the night and bring me to bed, angrier than ever. "Why didn't you leave then?" you ask. That's a hard question to answer. Almost any routine, no matter how horrendous, starts to appear normal after a while. During the day we were a regular family, the kids did regular things, I got up and got dressed and went to work. Deep inside I knew I couldn't carry that knot in my stomach forever – but, for now, it was one foot in front of the other.

There was never any doubt that David was capable of killing me. He even talked about it – described it in detail. He would never do anything obvious, anything that would point the finger at him. He'd get upset at characters in a movie who shot or stabbed their wives in front of witnesses – how amateurish. His way was quiet and unexpected. He said he could wait years if he had to for the right moment. Then, when no one expected it, when no one was thinking about it, when he wasn't even around – it would happen. An accident. No warning bruises, no public scenes, no witnesses. That was his style.

David had worked as a social worker for several years and understood the significance of injuries and bruises. He was proud to be above that. Picking Michael up, turning him upside down and shaking him didn't leave marks. Constantly berating and threatening the boys didn't leave welts. Shoving me off chairs and hitting the wall beside my face didn't leave injuries. Throwing Stephanie on the bed didn't leave bruises (except for a split lip that no one noticed). Unfortunately, the emotional toll isn't always recognized until it's too late.

One evening the family was at the dinner table, having a reasonably good time. We were eating steak – T-bone probably. David finished before I did and he took his plate and emptied the bones and gristle off his plate on to mine (while I was still eating). He did it quietly, without breaking the flow of conversation, and I'm certain no one noticed. That act said everything that needed to be said about what he thought of me – I was simply a receptacle for his trash. That stands out as one of my worst memories.

In the end, it was Michael who brought me to my senses. When he was 14 he asked me what it felt like to smoke pot. I told him I didn't know because I had never smoked it, but it was probably like getting drunk, and who needs that? He said some friends at school told him it helps you feel relaxed – and *he had never felt relaxed one day in his life*.

His words exploded in my head like a bomb. How could I have been so stupid as to think that the environment in which my kids had been raised had not affected them deeply? What made me think I was the only victim and I could afford to be a martyr? How could bearing this cross be a good thing for anyone? I knew what I had to do. I had failed to protect my family and now I had to save them. I wasn't sure when or how, but I knew I had to leave David.

I didn't know how this was going to go but I had to prepare myself. I wondered if I was strong enough and if the kids were going to suffer more. I worried about everyone – even David – because he was a victim too. He had grown up in a terribly violent environment, one in which every family get-together ended with the adults in drunken brawls and the children cowering under tables in fear. He told me he had seen his father break a chair over his mother's head and once he shoved her out of a moving car. When his sister was 13, his father had knocked her unconscious because he caught her talking with a boy. David had helped his mother pick her up and put her in bed. The reality was, David had accomplished what he wanted. He *was* better than his father.

It was 10 months between my telling David that we had to separate and his permanently leaving the home. He left and returned three times during that period, alternating between fits of rage and tearful promises to change. It was a very tense time. The kids were confused. I still had not told anyone, friends or family, anything. Outward appearances continued. Finally, in 1977, about a week before Christmas, David left.

The next two years were a nightmare. David's threats to kill me became more concrete. He told Michael he had bought a gun. He called me day and night and tormented me while I sat on the floor crying, too afraid to hang up on him. He had a key to "his" house and I was too afraid to have the locks changed. He threatened to take the kids and I would never see them again. He had a hunting rifle in the house and I took it to a good friend and asked her to keep it. I told her that if I was killed in an accident, she should let the police know it was murder.

I also called my mother and told her the kids and I might have to leave the house in a hurry and could we come to her. Imagine going from complete silence about your married life to telling your mother your life is in danger. She was a smart woman and I'm sure knew something was wrong....but not this. We agreed on a spot in the side yard where she and my dad would put a spare key to their house.

About a year after our separation, David filed for a divorce. It was important that he be the one to file – he would not have tolerated having his wife file against him. My attorney wanted to move very aggressively and I soon realized that her actions were putting me in more danger. I didn't want more contention and conflict; I wanted peace. So, I let my attorney go and told David I would agree to any reasonable settlement he and his attorney wrote up.

I signed the agreement and also signed a waiver so that I wouldn't have to appear at the divorce hearing. I thought it better that David and I not have face-to-face contact at that time. I couldn't risk a confrontation. David told me later that it had all gone very well. In fact, the judge commended him for being present and for arriving at such a generous settlement.

The truth is that the first time David left, he bought a new silver Camaro with red upholstery. The second time he left, he took an extended vacation to Spain. I, on the other hand, went to my credit union to borrow money – a total of $7,000 (a lot of money in those days) just to keep going. One month, he refused to give me any child support money; another month his check bounced, causing all of my checks to bounce. I kept all the bills; his only debt was his new car. I even paid off the swimming pool he had put in as a parting gift to the kids. I streamlined my budget, cutting out anything non-essential like the automatic contribution to United Way that came out of my paycheck. For a few winter months, we didn't turn on the heater and I remember Christopher sitting in the living room wearing a sweatshirt with the hood up and shivering.

Many times during our marriage and after we separated, I suggested to David that we go to counseling but he always scoffed at the idea. When he started writing me letters vowing to change and promising me the world, I went to a therapist with one question: is it possible for someone with his history to change? She thought it was possible but only with intensive, long-term psychotherapy. I told her it didn't seem right that he wasn't there to present his side; how could she advise me if she only had my version of the story. She said I reminded her of a previous client who had expressed the same concern. The woman had bruises around her neck from her husband choking her. That woman is now dead.

At some point, David did seek therapy. I think he was frightened by his own behavior and his thoughts of doing me harm. He told me much later that he had a team of therapists so someone would be available to him around the clock. He was to call them any time the idea of hurting me came to his mind. They told him not to see me when he picked up the kids for a visit and not to visit in our home. They warned that the court hearing could potentially trigger an explosive event. In a controlled setting, they had him go through the motions of killing me to release tension.

The divorce was final in November of 1979. Things did get better after that although there were plenty of tense moments. Around 1984, David decided to move into the family home (he still had a key) to be a father to the boys. So, Margaret and I moved into a two-bedroom apartment near St. Christopher's Church in West Covina (Stephanie was in a Regional Center group home). I loved that little apartment even though it resembled grad students' housing – a mismatch of furniture, dishes, etc. For the first time, I felt completely free and loved having a place that was truly my own. I don't know what happened between David and the boys during that period but one day Michael came to the apartment with all his belongings in his car and announced his father had kicked him out of the house. He meant it literally as he showed us the bruises on his legs. After nine months, David announced that he was moving out of the house and Margaret and I returned.

As hard as it may be to imagine, David and I made several reconciliation attempts during the ten years following the divorce. During these periods, he was romantic and attentive and a new man. This lasted throughout the chase period. But as soon as he thought the chase was over and he had me, he reverted to his controlling, demanding self. I saw this change of behavior take place from one day to the next. When it became abundantly clear that my fantasy of a happy family was never going to materialize and that what David really wanted was me under his control *and* whatever or whoever else he desired, it was finally truly over. Shortly after that, he remarried (surprisingly, not his longstanding romantic interest).

While David was married, I felt the safest. My therapist had told me his fixation on me would not end until he found another focus. So as long as he was married, I didn't have to look over my shoulder. I had no trouble chatting with him or sharing a joke and was delighted when he and his wife had a son. However, his marriage didn't last and I returned to looking over my shoulder.

My current relationship with David is tenuous. We have five children and there are plenty of occasions when we need to be at some function together. This will be the case for the rest of our lives. I would like very much to relax around him, to be friendly and pleasant, to talk and laugh. But I can't. It would be far too easy for him to misinterpret the slightest look or gesture or kind word and think there was something rekindling between us. I have to be aloof and cold, avoiding physical proximity as much as possible. I still have the occasional nightmare to remind me what it was like to be truly afraid.

To my children, grandchildren, and future generations I say: I did not write this to make David the bad guy or to have you hate him. Even during the worst of times, I saw him as a victim and believed he didn't have a chance to be different given his childhood experiences. I may still be afraid of him but I harbor no ill will. I don't want you to either. What I do want is for you to understand the history of violence in your family and that, given the right stresses and circumstances; you may exhibit some of this behavior. Do everything you can to educate yourselves and seek professional help at the first inkling that there may be a problem. And, if you find yourselves in an abusive relationship, run. You don't have to be angry and you can forgive if you want but don't hesitate, don't rationalize, don't be a martyr, don't try to fix it – just run. Please.

XIII

THE ARREST

The 1960's was a remarkable decade. No, I'm not referring to hippies, pot smoking, flower power, Woodstock, or even the Beatles. This was the decade of the space race, the Woolworth lunch counter sit-ins, the desegregation of public schools in the south, anti-Vietnam War protests, the sexual revolution via the Pill, and the assassinations of President John F. Kennedy, Martin Luther King, Jr., and Robert F. Kennedy.

As news programs on television displayed the sights and sounds of peaceful demonstrations and marches across the country, I longed to be among the throngs of young people who were openly expressing their opposition to war and to civil rights injustices. Protest was in my heart and I cheered those who risked incarceration, even assault, for standing up for righteousness. It was not meant for me, however. The 1960's was the decade I was having babies and more mundane activities occupied my time. It wasn't until 1986 that I had the opportunity to take a public stand. That was the year I was arrested.

It started when a work colleague mentioned a conference sponsored by the Interfaith Center to Reverse the Arms Race in Pasadena. I recalled the paralyzing fear of the A-bomb after

Hiroshima and then the Soviet Union testing that started in 1949. The arms race was on and accounts of possible nuclear destruction were terrifying. We practiced *duck and cover* exercises at school and wished we could afford to build bomb shelters in our backyards. I remember praying before taking baths, asking God for no bombs for the next 30 minutes because I didn't want to be found naked.

At the conference, we received literature on a nonviolent action to take place May 31 – June 2, 1986 at the Nevada Test Site. It was sponsored by the American Peace Test (APT) and appeared to be a well-organized and safe operation. I had missed out on opportunities to express my opposition to war and to nuclear testing in my youth. I was not going to miss out again in middle age.

A friend and I drove to Las Vegas where the APT managed a packed schedule. On June 1, they provided mandatory nonviolence training and held a comprehensive briefing on site, scenario, and legal issues. They made sure participants knew exactly what they were doing and were prepared for the consequences. The Department of Energy and local law enforcement had been notified of the protest. Everything was completely transparent.

On June 2, we were driven to the entrance of the Nevada Test Site. We were about a mile from the site's main gate and could not see the buildings but buses carrying employees passed in front of us. It was a desolate desert area marked by a couple of porta-potties. Experienced protesters brought blankets to sit on, bottles of water, and chunks of bread and cheese. When I realized the porta-potties had no soap (hand sanitizers were not yet available to consumers), the bread and cheese were being passed from person to person to break off a piece, and the water bottles made the rounds, I was happy I had my own water and protein bars. I must have looked like a snob but, in the end, nobody really cared.

We sang, waved at employees on their way to work (many of whom waved back) and waited for Nye County Sheriff's officers to arrive. The mood was expectant and tense. Then came the moment we were waiting for. With arms locked, we marched down the road and crossed a white no-trespassing line. A few hardy protesters broke rank and ran towards the fence that surrounds the site but were held back by guards on off-road motorcycles. What was running through my head at the time was not that we were breaking a law but that we were upholding an intrinsic right to live without the devastation of war. It was exhilarating!

The event was completely nonviolent. Police placed light plastic handcuffs on us as we were arrested for trespassing on federal land. They took us by bus to the police station in Beatty where we were processed in an orderly, respectful manner. We were released and told we would be notified of subsequent proceedings. Ours was the largest group ever arrested there – 149 of us – and included Anne Druyan, author and wife of astrophysicist, Carl Sagan.

We did not go to trial until almost four months later. It was decided that a few defendants would appear in court and the rest of us would be tried *in absentia.* We assumed a conviction in the lower court and the plan was to take the case on appeal to the District Court. Ultimately, the goal was to try future Test Site defendants in Federal Court.

The attorneys involved were diligent about keeping all of us informed on the trial's progress. They described the expert testimony as compelling. Planning and preparation for nuclear war is a violation of international law and the Nuremberg principles give individuals the right to take necessary action to prevent such violations. Research on cancer rates of persons living downwind of the Test Site indicates statistically significant increases in the expected incidences of certain cancers within this group. No level of radioactive exposure is safe, whether tests are conducted above or below ground.

Nevertheless, we lost this battle and on September 29, 1986, we were found guilty of the misdemeanor charge of trespassing on federal land. The case did not go up on appeal. I paid a fine of $150.00 plus a $10.00 administrative assessment fee.

My activism did not end then. I continued participating in rallies against nuclear testing, giving speeches and promoting letter-writing to legislators. I was a member of the Catholic Peace Coalition and the Nuclear Freeze of San Gabriel Valley. I was also co-founder of a Peace and Justice Committee at my local Catholic Church. The committee did not last long, however, because we received no support (and perhaps a little hostility) from our very conservative, Irish pastor.

Even though I actively protested government actions that put us in jeopardy of war, I'm not generally an anti-government person. I did consider myself "anti-establishment" during the Vietnam War and I was not alone; it was hard to find anyone who supported it. Unfortunately, military personnel got the brunt of our despair. All too often, they came home, wounded and confused, to unwelcoming and angry crowds. The anger was displaced, of course, and in time we as a nation realized what we had done and vowed never to treat our men and women in service with such disrespect. Today, military personnel are revered and hailed as heroes. No opportunity is lost to celebrate them and show our gratitude.

I think that's a good thing. But I also believe we are acting on misguided conclusions. There is a lesson to be learned from the Vietnam War, to be sure. But the lesson is not that we should cheer when our troops return home. The lesson is that we should not go to war to start with. Then we wouldn't have thousands of men and women coming home maimed and with PTSD. And we wouldn't have to worry about how we're going to welcome them.

So I say, stand up for what you believe is right, even if it hurts a little. I have seen signs of activism in my family. Margaret joined me in a protest march against the Gulf War in 1990. More recently, she and Vincent (and their partners) participated in Women's Marches following the Trump inauguration. It isn't always easy to stand up for what you believe. Sometimes it's even hard to discern *what* it is you believe. There are so many influences: cable news, social media, favorite entertainers. First you decide what's important to you; then you decide if it's important enough for you to be vocal about it. Answer the basic question: what kind of a world do you want to leave your grandchildren? Don't be afraid to run against the current or lose a few friends or have people raise an eyebrow. If it's right, it's right.

Local woman faces court in nuke trespass protest

By Renee Wallace
Staff Writer

"I have a commitment to my children and grandchildren. I want to have a world to leave to them," said Madeline Olea of La Puente.

Olea, who works with abused and neglected children at MacLaren Hall in El Monte, was arrested June 2 at a nuclear test site in Nevada. She has pleaded innocent to charges of trespassing on federal land. She is one of 149 protesters arrested in a two-day period.

"I had to make a choice. I had been a believer; now I had to be a doer," the 45-year-old, mother of five said.

Her involvement started May 14 at a conference sponsored by the Interfaith Center to Reverse the Arms Race of Pasadena.

"I made up my mind then I had to do something. I just needed a chance," she said.

Her opportunity to show her opposition to nuclear weapons came when the government conducted an underground nuclear explosion. Olea was one of 315 protesters demonstrating at the site.

"Civil disobedience was a choice, you didn't have to do it, but I felt I had to," she said.

Olea, who is divorced, said her children, ages 17 to 24, were very supportive of her decision to participate in the protest.

"Actually they were very excited about it and very interested in what was going to happen," she said.

"I did it because I want them to be able to live life free from the threat of nuclear destruction," she added.

Olea supervises the filing of court petitions on behalf of juveniles who

Madeline Olea

have been severely neglected or abused.

"I deal with violence every day. I feel obilgated to oppose it," she commented.

Olea's trial probably will be held in September or October.

96

XIV

A CAREER

I always knew I'd be a "somebody." Not rich, to be sure, or famous, or powerful; but someone who was reasonably well educated, who could think for herself, who was a good citizen, and who made some positive contribution somewhere. As a child and teenager, I had lofty dreams – a saintly nun, a child psychologist, an attorney in East LA championing the rights of Latinos. When I took piano lessons (for a whole year) I saw myself playing in Carnegie Hall. Too bad I never thought it was necessary to practice.

I went to work in March of 1969, when Michael was six years and Margaret was six months. We hired an undocumented immigrant who lived in during the week and watched the kids. I was determined not to rush my children every morning to a day care center, putting them in an unfamiliar surrounding while I worked. I wanted them home to nap in their own beds and play in their own yard. We didn't know much about early brain development or sensory stimulation in those days. I thought day care places simply warehoused children so their indulgent parents could both work. I feel differently now and believe the right day care facility can stimulate early leaning, quench natural curiosity, and facilitate socialization. All I provided was a person who took physical care of my children but couldn't communicate with them in their own language. Big mistake.

But – something wonderful happened when I went to work. The value of my education clicked like never before. My coworkers were all college educated, interesting people with whom I could engage in intelligent conversations and, more amazingly, who thought I was interesting and whose opinion they respected. Not that I had a lot in common with my early coworkers. Most were just out of college, single, and using the Department of Public Social Services (DPSS) as a steppingstone to something better. At that time, DPSS hired people with a BA in any major, so interests ran long and wide. Most young people worked a year or two and then found something in their field. But for the time being, we were social workers who, initially, processed and managed public assistance programs and, later, provided services to abused and neglected children and their families. It felt good – I was a somebody.

I learned to live with chronic guilt; the guilt suffered by every working mother with small children. I felt in my gut my children had many needs that only I could (should) meet. I knew they were my primary responsibility and my primary joy. But I saw no way out. We couldn't manage on David's salary alone, especially if we were going to build a decent home in which to raise them. And I had worried about the person I was becoming when all I had were four walls around me and five babies clinging to me. I didn't realize it then but I was depressed and angry. I was totally dependent on a husband who believed children and housekeeping were women's work. My self-esteem plummeted; I felt worthless with no hope for the future, certainly no more lofty dreams.

This was not a healthy environment in which to raise children. Stay-at-home moms today have many avenues in which to socialize and feel part of their community. Women have options and many choose to delay motherhood until after they've established themselves in the workforce as valued human beings. They bring confidence and self-esteem into the role of motherhood. I had none of that. Going to work when my children were so young no doubt hurt them, but I may have hurt them more by limiting my life to those four walls and continuing in a state of darkness. As a working mom, I was still stressed out of my mind, but I now walked around with my head held high and that had to count for something.

In my early years as social worker, I investigated child abuse referrals. At that time, we could keep a case open as long as we thought necessary. There were few forms to fill out and rare was the child taken into protective custody. The field of child abuse/neglect was new and we were pioneers. This means we really didn't know what we were doing – we were writing the script as we went along. Our only basis of authority was the 1962 revolutionary *Battered-Child Syndrome* by Kempe, et.al. We devoured training by The American Humane Association. We dictated our case notes free-form style hoping they would be approved by our supervisors (who knew little more than we did).

Without legal guidelines or support from law enforcement, we may still have accomplished our best social work in those days. That may have been the case for me. In March, 1971, I was monitoring a family closely - the mother was diagnosed paranoid-schizophrenic, the stepfather was disabled and considerably older. The eldest child, a 10-year-old I'll call Johnny, had been ill with the mumps and was unable to come to the living room so I could see him. The mom blocked my way into his bedroom and, against my better judgment, I moved her aside and found Johnny lying in filthy bed sheets with dirt and secretions crusted on his face and barely able to talk. I knew I had to get him medical attention. The family had no telephone and this was decades before cell phones so I left the home and drove to the nearest pay phone. I called the local Sheriff's Dept. (no 911 back then) and described what I found, hoping for assistance in securing an ambulance. The dispatcher simply said, "You're the social worker – what do you want us to do?" I called my supervisor and told her I was driving the family to the hospital.

I don't know how the stepfather and I were able to get Johnny into the back of my VW bus. The stepdad sat with Johnny and I put the mother and her 8-month old baby (who was wearing no diapers) in the front with me. As we drove, the mother grabbed my gear shift, threatening to crash the car. I held her arm while the stepfather wrapped his around her from behind.

At the hospital, I introduced myself as the family's social worker. The doctor came out to see me before examining Johnny and told me angrily that, under no circumstances, did he want to get involved (in any court procedure). A nurse told me she did want to get involved and I asked her to simply document everything she saw in her notes. Nurses cleaned Johnny's arms with alcohol on a washcloth so they could take blood and insert an IV. Lying in clean sheets for the first time in who knows how long, Johnny whispered to me that he just wanted to go home (a common response of abused children).

A short time later, the same doctor came out to see me but the look on his face had changed. He said Johnny had a ruptured spleen and they were sending him to Children's Hospital in LA via ambulance and with a police escort. He added that, if Johnny lived, I had saved his life. Johnny did recover – from surgery and sepsis and stress ulcers – but only after months of hospitalization and rehabilitation. He and his siblings were later adopted by an aunt.

My experience in this case was not different from that of countless other social workers. By chance, I was acknowledged for having saved a life but social workers across the nation do that on a daily basis. It's challenging to quantify something that didn't happen – children that didn't die or weren't physically harmed or weren't emotionally wrecked. Child protection workers get a bad rap always, but I know workers who labored into the night looking for runaway teens, or came to work really sick because a court report was due, or knocked on doors even armed police wouldn't touch, or talked to young children about unspeakable acts, or spent the night in the office with a troubled youth because no placement would take him. I have tremendous respect for child welfare (CPS) workers everywhere and I'm proud to have been one.

Shortly after I started working, DPSS separated public assistance from child welfare. When the big test came for the newly created position of Children's Services Worker (CSW), we all studied like we were back in college. Happily, I passed the test and was promoted to CSW II in December of 1971.

In 1972, I volunteered for a pilot unit in which we handled a variety of cases, including those that required comprehensive reports on whether a child should become a Dependent of the Court. There was structure in the Dependency process (as opposed to Protective Services) because that function had previously been handled by the Probation Department and was spelled out in the California Welfare & Institutions Code. However, it wasn't until 1980 that federal law PL 96-272 defined how child welfare and adoption cases would be handled and four more years before LA County went into full implementation.

The CSW III position was offered for the first time in 1973. I scored high on the general list and #1 on the Spanish-Speaking list. When the office Deputy called to offer me the position in Pomona, I declined, telling him I didn't want to go that far from home. My supervisor was shocked at my response and lectured me about never refusing a promotion. So I took the offer, pushing back the additional guilt brought on by a longer commute. Instead of a 12-minute drive to West Covina, I now drove 30 minutes to Pomona. On the plus side, my colleagues there were more my age, with young families, and many friendships I was fortunate to form continue to the present day.

I was only in Pomona for three years but I did see positive changes in our relationship with law enforcement. On one occasion, early on, when I called Pomona PD to report an infant in a crack house, I got the old, "Do what you have to do." And then there was the time I was met at a client's door by paramedics, fire fighters and police officers. They collectively cheered that I was there and proceeded to leave me alone with a mother lying on the sofa in a catatonic state and her scared-to-death children. However, a couple of years later the Juvenile Detective from Pomona PD willingly accompanied me to a home in which a 4-year old held his mentally ill mother's face in his hands and begged her to feed him.

After Pomona, I transferred to the Rancho (Los Amigos) Unit, a unit that handled the placement and supervision of medically fragile children. Assignment to a specialized unit had its perks (lower caseloads) but the emotional burden could take its toll. We worked with children left quadriplegic following horrific brain and spinal cord injuries; children in wheel chairs with disorders like Spina Bifida and Cerebral Palsy; children born with no limbs. On the plus side, we were privileged to work with the foster parents who loved and cared for these children.

One of my Rancho clients was a baby born with a rare lung disorder that stunted her physical growth and mental development. There were few documented cases of children with her condition and none had lived past the age of four. The foster mother cherished the baby and took the biological mother under her wing, despite language and distance barriers. We all prepared for her death even while we did what we could to give her some quality of life. She lived two years.

I got the call from the foster mom late one night that the baby had died. I arrived at the home before the biological mother but the Bishop from the Mormon Temple attended by the foster family was already there. The foster mother, her biological teenage children, and I took turns holding the dead baby, still wrapped in a blanket, as we said our goodbyes. When the (Mormon) mortuary hearse arrived, the Bishop asked the drivers to stand by until the mother got there. She was then given private time to hold her baby for the last time. The child was not placed in the back of the hearse as is usual. Instead, one of the drivers carried the baby in his arms as they drove away, leaving that as the final image of the baby for the two mothers. At the funeral, the Bishop and others deliberately spoke slowly so that I could translate for the mom. I'll never forget the compassion shown to the mother by the Mormon clergy and congregation.

My next assignment was to a unit located in El Monte at MacLaren Children's Center (closed in 2003). Social workers in this unit determined, based on a petition request or police report, whether there was sufficient cause to proceed with the court process. If so, we prepared a petition and detention report for court the next day; if not, we released the child. This means we had one working day in which to contact parents, witnesses and interested parties and talk to the child. If the child was placed at MacLaren, we could see the child in person, often in tandem with the juvenile detective on the case. Depending on how many children were taken into custody two business days prior, we each handled two to seven cases every day. Tuesdays were our heavy days because we were assigned children taken into custody on Friday, Saturday and Sunday. There were about 10 of us.

That job was the hardest and the easiest of my social work career. Hardest because it was demanding and stressful from the moment we sat at our desks in the morning. We were super sleuths digging up every possible clue necessary to make a life-changing decision for a child and his/her family. And, it had to be wrapped up before the end of the day so it could be waiting for court personnel the next morning (imagine the overtime worked by our clerical staff). Keep in mind, we had no computers, no faxes, no email. Everything was hand written by social workers, typed by clerks, and delivered by mail couriers.

This was also the easiest job because when we went home at night, we were done. Absolutely nothing trailed over to the next day; we could relax and enjoy our evenings, weekends, and vacations without worrying if one of our cases had blown up or dreading the messages and alerts piling up on our desks. This perk provided some balance to an otherwise horrendous and challenging job.

One of the saddest cases in which I felt I provided some justice concerned a Mexican immigrant family with two children: a toddler and an infant. The father worked long hours in a *tortilleria* for less than minimum wage. When the infant came down with diarrhea, the mother gave him rice water to drink – a common home remedy among Latino families. The infant became dehydrated very quickly and by the time the family made it to County Hospital, the baby could not be saved. Because the infant would probably have lived had he been medically treated earlier, hospital staff contacted the police and they took the sibling into protective custody. While hospital staff and the police followed legal protocol, I could not ask these devastated and grieving parents to attend a court hearing for one child while they made funeral arrangements for another. I was able to release the toddler to his parents and request that a field social worker help the family with funeral plans and make other appropriate referrals.

When the long-awaited Supervising Children's Services Worker exam was given, I didn't hesitate to accept the position at IDC. My co-supervisor and I decided he would be responsible for all "desk" functions and I would review all petitions before they were submitted. This worked well for us and we were proud of our cohesive group. Then, while I was out on vacation, a notice went out announcing a Management Trainee spot at Department Headquarters. My co-supervisor submitted both of our names. When I got the call from Headquarters offering me one of the five spots, I didn't know what the Director's assistant was talking about. "What is a Management Trainee and is this something I should want?" I asked.

The idea of being part of "management" was odious. Hadn't I believed, like every good worker, that management's job was to make workers' lives miserable? I swallowed my pride and accepted the offer – partly out of curiosity, partly because I liked change, and largely because I was tickled to be chosen. Initially, I felt intimidated by the prospect of receiving a crash course on the inner workings of several department sections at Headquarters within a year's time. Not that I wasn't up to the challenge but deep inside I feared the other trainees were far more social and engaging than I was and I would come out looking like chopped liver next to them. And, besides, at 47, I was the oldest of the group.

I gained confidence as we rotated through various departmental sections – finance, budgets, policy, personnel, facilities management. I gave my best to each section, drawing on my social work experience and making sense of what it took to make the Department of Children Services run (at that time it was a 4,000 employee Department). While my focus was on learning all I could, no one was more surprised than I when I met with success after success. The mystique of Headquarters evaporated before me; I discovered that program folks did care about child safety; I learned it was possible to hold very divergent views from top management officials and still fully support the mission of the department; and I came to appreciate that I could do any job that was asked of me. That was a year of real discovery!

When the year of training ended, I was assigned to the position of Deputy Regional Administrator in the El Monte office. It was not a true promotion (with a salary increase) because I was still classified as a supervisor, but I didn't care. I now had my dream job. I was responsible for an office of about 100 employees who provided the full spectrum of child welfare services. My boss, the Regional Administrator, was located in another office and gave me the autonomy to run my office my way. The office was large enough to be a significant challenge but small enough that I could interact personally with staff and get involved in individual cases. I worked long hours including weekends and holidays. The timing was perfect for me to do that; my kids were young adults and could take care of themselves. I was now married to my job and I loved every minute of it.

The love affair only lasted eleven months. At a management meeting, the Bureau Chief and head of regional operations asked me if I wanted to be the Regional Administrator (RA) over Region III. I asked, "Do you think I'm ready?" She smiled and I had the job. At that time, the county (with a population of nine million) was divided into six regions for operational purposes. Region III included two offices and several specialized units, with close to 300 employees providing services to about 7,000 children. I knew there were competent deputy regional managers in that region who had been doing the job for many years and were seen as next in line for the RA position. I also knew the Belvedere office (regional headquarters) in Region III had a reputation for rebellious employees and a strong anti-management sentiment. I had a strong inkling that my appointment had hidden political implications and my ethnicity could certainly be seen as an asset, maybe even a ploy. This only made me more determined to prove I could do the job and do it well.

My years in Region III were as satisfying as they were frustrating. A top priority was to gain the trust of staff in Belvedere while making it clear I was in charge. I also had to convince the union we could accomplish more by working together (easy for me because I always aligned on the labor side of the table). My open-door policy was sincere; I believed any problem could be resolved if we just talked about it; I answered all questions thrown at me in private and during general staff meetings; and I promised I would never lie ("you will know what I know," I said). My motto hung on my office wall: *The role of management is to create an environment in which workers can do their job.*

Within a year, the tension in Belvedere had dissipated. Staff smiled at me more. Problem employees chose to leave. General staff meetings became enjoyable gatherings with lively discussion rather than assemblies for the disgruntled to vent anger, hurl accusations, and make demands. I felt like I could remove my armored vest.

My armored vest always lay close to me, however. I needed it again when a supervisor in Belvedere was arrested for molesting his grandchildren and some of their friends. The story became a hot topic on the 6:00 and 11:00 news for weeks. Staff walked around dazed. The regional deputy over the supervisor was an internationally recognized expert on child sexual abuse and he was consumed with guilt that he didn't see any signs. I feared the worst – that the accused supervisor had also molested children in his or in his unit's caseloads – but, thankfully, my investigation and one conducted by personnel (internal affairs) showed no evidence of that. Apparently, he was able to compartmentalize his behavior and knew that work was off limits.

There's no question I came very close to losing my job over this scandal. When something of this magnitude gets the attention of the Board of Supervisors, the Children's Services Commission and the media, someone's head has to roll. It needs to be someone high enough on the chain of command for it to mean something but not necessarily the people at the very top. As it turned out, the Director and the Bureau Chief of the Department were on their way out anyway, for a variety of other reasons, and the Bureau Chief quietly and unobtrusively took the bullet for me. The Belvedere supervisor pleaded *no contest* to the sexual abuse and was sentenced to several years in prison.

The year 1990 was a significant one for me and for the Department. The California Department of Social Services issued a Notice of Non-Compliance to the Department and threatened to take over child welfare responsibilities (they had already assumed responsibility for foster home licensing). A retired judge was appointed as Interim Manager for six months while the Department developed its Corrective Action Plan and a search was launched for a new Director.

Then I got the call from Headquarters. I was asked to accept a special assignment as consultant and advisor to the interim head of regional operations (she had not come up the social work ranks). This was a six-month assignment at Headquarters in which I would represent the social work/service delivery perspective on all issues relative to the department's reorganization and would be part of the Executive Management Team that developed the Corrective Action Plan. To sweeten the deal, they offered to assign an interim regional manager to cover for me in my absence. I said no.

I did think about it, though. Was I committing political suicide by refusing the assignment? I couldn't take the chance that I might be sent to the department's proverbial basement to count paper clips. I called back and countered that I would accept the assignment if I could maintain my position in Region III during the six months and if I was guaranteed my return to the Region after the special assignment terminated. That done, I embarked on the most strenuous six months of my career.

Much of the stress during this period came from the nature and the amount of work that needed to be accomplished: the reviewing, revising and reissuing of departmental policies and procedures and the creation and implementation of new forms to conform to State requirements. But, also, the strained relationships with the other Regional Administrators (all much more experienced and tenured than I) that resulted from the perception that I was given a perk or special recognition weighed heavily on me. And then there was the fact that I was, by nature, quiet and reserved and found it hard to speak up in a large group of articulate, vociferous folks. I was not a fighter.

I was relieved and eager to return to my region, which, like the other regions, was besieged with orders related to compliance with State regulations. Monthly reports were published showing compliance stats for each region, unit and individual worker. I had no problem with the need for accountability; for example, at my first general staff meeting in Belvedere I was asked what was my top priority and I wrote on the chalkboard "*see the children.*" But now, the Home Call requirement became a joke and workers laughed about drive-by home calls in which any dependent child spotted anywhere (like a Christmas party) by any social worker could be written up as having been "seen". The home call was no longer the most important assessment tool for determining child safety. It was simply a hash mark.

My displeasure with the Department grew as more pressure was put on regional staff to meet standards in assembly line fashion rather than by focusing on the individual needs and wellbeing of children and their families. For Regional Administrators, the compliance reports became all-consuming, dictating our futures and our salaries (we were on performance-based pay).

In the middle of this, I faced the Regional Administrator's worst nightmare – an infant under court supervision was returned home and then died at the hands of a parent. Life stood still as social workers were interviewed and files were reviewed. Then, there I was on the 6:00 and 11:00 TV news defending the Department's actions. Fortunately, I had the perfect defense: my social worker had recommended continued placement for the baby but the Dependency Court Judge had listened to the pleas of the parents' attorney and had ordered the infant to be released home. Sadly, I don't remember mourning the death of a child as much as rejoicing over being able to pass the buck of guilt.

Clearly, my dream job had turned into a nightmare. I did not agree with the philosophy or management style of the Department's new Director. Most importantly, I could not look my staff in the eye and assure them everything was going to be all right. Something had to change and then, in 1992, out of dark skies came a silver lining. In response to severe budgetary constraints, the County was offering what they called an Early Separation Plan (ESP) for managers. It was a financially attractive offer but a difficult one for a 52-year-old with only 23 years of County employment (you had to work at least 25 years to receive full health care coverage). Was I ready to retire?

I decided to not think of it as retirement but, rather, as a bold move to the next chapter of my life. My children were adults and I was unencumbered; it was time to think about what was good for me. For the last couple of years, I had fantasized about going back to school for a graduate degree. Here it was, August, and school would start in October. I had to hurry. I called the Deans of the Social Work/Social Welfare Departments at USC and UCLA and made my pitch. UCLA said yes first and within a few short weeks I was sitting in a UCLA auditorium surrounded by young, fresh, hopeful faces. It had been sad to say goodbye to my dedicated social work staff, but it felt good to say hello to the new world of academia.

XV

ACADEMIA & LIFE

I was happy and comfortable in the Masters of Social Welfare (MSW) program at UCLA but it was not without surprises. I knew I would probably be the oldest student in the program but I was a bit taken aback when I found myself older than most of the professors. And beyond that, I came in wearing my practitioner hat only to discover some tension between practice and academia. At first I thought that for me it was just concrete issues, like the facts that my professional style of writing was very different from that expected of a student and that some lessons were strangely contrary to my experience (e.g. CPS workers don't have the luxury of "establishing rapport" before making critical and immediate decisions).

Then it dawned on me that academia is not the real world; it's a world in which you discuss theoretical issues and talk about people and families in the generic. In the work world, children have names and they live within families and you have hands-on responsibility for them. In the academic world, children are part of a theoretical construct and you don't see their faces. The two disciplines are not always in sync and there's a layer of distrust on the part of each for the other.

Still, after so many years in the field, I thoroughly enjoyed the academic aspect of social welfare and decided to apply for the PhD program. I didn't necessarily expect to teach at the university level, but thought the degree would be helpful if I did any consulting. The truth is, I loved being a student. Not all faculty members agreed I was a good candidate, but with the help of Dr. Rosina Becera, I entered the doctoral program in October of 1994. I did not find the program difficult but it was extremely demanding. The perfect PhD student is young, spends the day on campus, and is immersed in his/her advisor's research. I was old, commuted 33 high-traffic miles from home, and was unable to engage a professor in my area of interest - how to break the cycle of violence (apparently, the existence of such a cycle had never been suggested by research).

The first two years went well; however, the doctoral degree was not meant to be mine. In August of 1996, my mother was diagnosed with terminal lung cancer and I took a leave of absence from school to care for her. She died in November so I resumed my classes quickly and got back into the rhythm of things easily. Then in March of 1997, my two youngest grandchildren, ages five and six, were court-ordered to my care. I took another leave of absence and for the next 20 months these grandchildren were my life. After they returned home, I found I had lost my momentum for school. The single-mindedness and dedication required of the doctoral program were gone. To be clear, I would not have written the script any other way. My grandchildren needed me at exactly that time and that was that. When life takes you in unplanned directions, you just go with it.

I hadn't worried much about finding work after retirement. In fact, while I was in graduate school, I had worked as a research associate for the UCLA Center for Child & Family Policy Research and I spent some time with the Child Welfare League of America. I didn't have to think long about my next step because, once again, my life found unmarked trails. In a series of gratuitous events, I bought a house in a rural area of the Pacific Northwest – 38 acres of pasture and woods reminding me of Switzerland. And, amazingly, while preparing for the big move, the local County Department of Human Services was posting an opening for a Program Manager for Adult and Children's Services.

What were the chances that a county position requiring an MSW and experience in exactly what I had done for 23 years would become available just as I was arriving? It did and it was mine. There were differences, of course, from my previous county job. I had no secretary, no staff assistant, no deputies – only an answering machine and a computer. And, I had the full spectrum of adult services as well as child welfare services, with approximately 15 social workers to cover the entire county (which mostly consists of small hamlets connected by mountainous roads that can be closed during severe winter storms). Some things were the same: social workers were criticized for every action they took or didn't take. And, I learned first-hand that State requirements were identical whether you worked for a large county with entire units dedicated to addressing them or for a small county with only the manager to handle them.

I had always planned to work in this small county for about five years and when I discovered I could retire after five years of employment, I was delighted. So in April of 2004, at the age of 63, I retired for the second time – this time permanently. For several years after that I was hired by the County for special projects related to State requirements and these kept me mentally engaged and were good for my pocket book but, pretty much, I was done.

Retirement is as scary as it is joyful. First, so much of your identity is wrapped up in your profession – what you "did" for a living; it takes a while to see yourself apart from that. Second, life is a series of milestones and retirement feels like you've come to the end of the road. Yes, there are bucket list activities to check off, but keep in mind that these are "before I die" activities. Third, you worry that you'll have enough money in the happy event you live a long time. I am very fortunate to have an adequate fixed income but there's no certainty my income will cover skilled nursing or memory care costs should I need them in the (far) future.

To my children I say – plan for your retirement now. The years will pass in a blink, trust me. The face of Social Security is changing and we don't know what it will look like when you need it. No longer can you live life for the present; every dollar you save today will be significant tomorrow. I expect my grandchildren and their children and grandchildren to heed the same advice. You'll know you're on the right track when watching your savings account grow is in itself a source of excitement and accomplishment. When putting a little money in the bank is as satisfying as buying the newest electronic trinket, you're there.

I would like to emphasize here the need, the value, the importance of education. I don't care what you do for a living or how much money you make, but I do care that you maximize the potential of your brain. I care that you learn to think for yourself; that you look at all sides of an issue; that you not be influenced by power or bling; that you welcome new ideas and challenge old ones; that you appreciate diversity; that you make a positive contribution someplace; that you be a somebody.

I'm a little like my Mom in this regard: I want this even more for women than I do for men. Listen, ladies, we have to work twice as hard and be twice as smart to make it in this world. Education is the great equalizer. I'll go so far as to say that we have a duty and obligation to pursue as much of it as life will allow. If you decide to stay home, as a stay-at-home mom or because you can afford a life of luxury, don't let that be the end of it. As soon as you can, get out in the world and do something. You're not meant to just occupy space; you're meant to accomplish and to serve.

All of you reading this: know that this applies to you. You're never too old; you're never too busy; it's never too late. Get a certificate or a license at a vocational or trade school. Go to college. Get a graduate degree. Aim for the PhD. Know that I'll be smiling at you when you do.

XVI

DYANE

Dyane is my friend but we are more different than we are alike: me a Catholic, she an atheist; me a part of a large family, she singularly devoted to her animals; me obsessed with order and neatness, she perfectly comfortable amidst chaos. But, we are very alike in the things that matter: philosophy of life, ideology, a shared work history. We laugh that we've lived together for so many years – much longer than my marriage.

Dyane started work with the Los Angeles County Department of Public Social Services in 1968. I came on board in 1969. For years, our paths crossed tangentially at trainings and departmental meetings. For many years, I was quietly focused on job and family so she probably paid little attention to me (she tells me now that when she first heard of me, she assumed I was Asian).

Dyane and I had more contact with each other when we were supervisors and had occasion to consult on cases that impacted both of our units. In the late 80's, we were working in the same region and discovered we had similar passions. We both loved roaming the local mountains – she mounted on her favorite horse and me hiking on my own two feet. Dyane rode Suni in

Griffith Park on a regular basis and had done some competitive trail rides. And, for years I had hiked the mountains behind Pasadena, Sierra Madre and Arcadia with friends, sometimes with a boyfriend, and even sometimes with my ex-husband during periods of attempted reconciliation.

As my work responsibilities increased, I found it harder to maintain a hiking routine. One day, I bemoaned to Dyane that I missed my jaunts in the mountains and she suggested I join her and Suni at Griffith Park. At first the idea of walking alongside a nearly 1,000-pound equine on a narrow trail seemed ludicrous, but I was desperate and relented. This was the start of a new relationship in which I trusted that Suni would not shove me off the trail and he gained respect for me as a worthy competitive mare. Sometimes he trotted in front of me only to stop and look back, bouncing with anticipation that I might gallop past him.

My friendship with Dyane grew as we explored Griffith Park's 53 miles of trails. We could leave the pressures of work behind and find humor in silly things. I saw firsthand the bond between Dyane and Suni and learned to appreciate equine intelligence. These excursions helped put life in perspective.

It was during this time that I had to make serious decisions about my family home. My divorce order specified that the house in which my children grew up was to be sold when the youngest child turned 18. Margaret was now 21 and my ex-husband was anxious to get his share of the equity. I couldn't afford to buy him out but neither could I afford a home mortgage on my salary alone. I started looking at condos and wondered what living alone would look like.

Dyane wasn't planning on moving but she did have a lifelong dream of having her horse in her backyard instead of boarded 15 miles away. Everyday without fail she drove to Burbank from Altadena and spent hours feeding, tending to, and cleaning around Suni. The foothill area of Altadena is horse country, so she kept her feelers out and fantasized about horse property.

In a series of happenstance events over the next few months, we ended up buying together an acre of horse property with a main house and detached studio in Altadena. An acre lot close to Los Angeles is rare. We considered ourselves fortunate to satisfy both of our wish lists: she could get companion horses for Suni and enjoy them 24/7, and I had plenty of room to host my children and family.

Not that there weren't hurdles to overcome. I had never lived with anyone to whom I wasn't related; she is a very private person who needs her space. We had a lawyer draw up a contract so it would be very clear how the property would be disposed of if something happened to one of us (mostly to protect my beneficiaries). It looked like a win-win situation. If it didn't work out, we'd sell the house and share the equity. We would re-assess it all when we retired.

As it turned out, our living arrangement worked out very well. Dyane and I got along fine and had plenty of private space. Dyane immediately got two more horses to keep Suni company. My mother was enchanted with my new home and called it "magical." The grandchildren loved visiting the horses and even shoveling manure. I thought more women who found themselves alone should consider similar non-traditional living arrangements.

It wasn't long before Dyane and I were fantasizing about real horse property – the kind with acres of pasture, pines and oaks, and miles of riding and hiking trails. It was like fantasizing about what we might do after winning the lottery, only the fantasy came true. Eight years later, we moved to a beautiful property in the country.

Many of our colleagues in Los Angeles County and in the rural county assumed we were a couple. Actually, that's a reasonable assumption; one that I myself might have made. At first, I tried desperately to dismiss the notion, I'm sure coming across as though I was protesting too much. Finally, I realized that people were going to believe what they wanted to believe and there was no need to explain anything. After all, I wasn't offended if someone thought I was Mormon (because I have a lot of kids) or if someone

116

mistook me as Portuguese (because there's a large population where I live); so, why should I be offended at being considered a lesbian (because I live with a woman)? I decided that, unless I was directly asked, I would not challenge anyone's opinion of my sexual orientation. Happily, aside from a few snickers and some curious looks, at no time have I felt discriminated against or belittled in any way.

So, why am I telling this story about Dyane? Because, as you read the letters I wrote to my grandchildren, you'll find her name mentioned more than a few times. She has become a member of the family, as anyone who has ever read one of my Christmas letters can attest. Life moves us in different directions based on good and bad decisions; I believe my decision to include Dyane in the story of my life was a good one.

XVII

LETTER TO HEATHER

December 22, 2012

Heather, I'm writing this letter to you on your 30th birthday to share with you my memories of your birth and early childhood. I can't believe my eldest grandchild is turning 30. It feels like only yesterday that I was at my desk at work and got a call from Michael, your dad, to tell me I was going to be a grandmother. Yes, he called me at work rather than tell me face-to-face. So, I did the only thing I could do – I put down the phone and soberly announced to my co-workers that I was going to be a grandma.

That doesn't mean it was easy for anybody. Both families were stunned. Your dad was just turning 20 and was completely unprepared to have a child. My fantasy had always been that you would be born to mature, nurturing parents who could provide you with a beautiful home and a loving environment. But life isn't fantasy – life is real. Your parents did the best they could and there was never any question that you were going to be loved and welcomed into the world. It touched my heart to see your dad going off to work with his bag lunch and his Lamaze book to study while he ate regardless of any teasing from his co-workers.

On December 22, 1982, your dad called me at work early to tell me he thought Michele, your mom, was in labor. I told him the first baby took a long time and there was no rush to call the doctor. "Just relax; it'll take a long time," I said calmly and went back to work. Good thing they didn't listen to me. They left for the hospital right away and barely made it. Your dad told me he was washing his hands getting ready to put his Lamaze training to use when he heard you cry. He was disappointed, of course, to not have participated in your birth, but he was thrilled with his baby girl. Actually, we were all thrilled. You were healthy and absolutely beautiful!

You were discharged from the hospital on Christmas Eve, tucked inside a large Christmas stocking. Your mom lived on the second floor of an apartment complex and the doctor advised her not to go up and down stairs for a week or so. So, the two of you came to my house. What a great Christmas gift! All your mom's and dad's relatives came to my house because that was where you were. Everyone wanted to hold you and we took turns, but with different levels of expertise in holding a baby – from an awkward uncle to a very experienced great-grandfather. But my favorite photo is of your two grandfathers carefully holding your baby carrier and looking at you with amazement. What a treasure!

Needless to say, Christmas of 1982 was a remarkable one and stands out in my mind as one of the best. You and your mom stayed at my house for a couple of weeks after you were born and it was good to see how much your parents loved you. I remember finding you fast asleep on your dad's chest as he lay on the sofa also fast asleep. You spent a lot of time at my house in those early years. When you were six months old, your dad walked around the back yard showing you plants and leaves and grass and having you touch them as he named them, "This is a leaf, this is a tree, this is grass ...."

We hadn't had a baby in the family for a long time and, as I think back, it's quite possible you may have been a little spoiled as a baby and toddler. We all loved holding you, playing with you, and showing you off. Your mom's family threw lavish birthday parties for you and the holidays were special with you around. Finally we had a child to make Christmas, Easter egg hunts and Halloween come to life. Your mom could always count on your looking adorable in a bunny costume (any costume, really) and she brought you over to my house so I could enjoy you and fuss over you.

But you didn't need a costume to look good. Simply dressed up for a special occasion, you could have been on a magazine cover. I knew that and proudly showed you off when I took you to work for Christmas parties and other occasions. They loved you at work and I took you often.

When you were two years old and your parents in their early twenties, you stayed with me for the weekend while your parents went to Las Vegas to get married. It was a special event for all of us although it was a quiet affair with just the two of them at the Hitching Post Wedding Chapel. You and I had a wonderful time back home shopping and hanging out.

It wasn't long before you demonstrated that you were not only beautiful but very smart. When you were about two, you and I made a birthday cake for my mother and were on the way to her house for a party. You commented about something we should have done or added to the cake (I don't remember exactly what) and I said that I wished we had thought of that earlier. You blew my mind when you answered, "That's okay, I'm just brainstorming." Seriously!

In early grade school, you and your mom moved to Temple City. Dyane and I lived in Altadena and were able to see you often. We even went to some of your open houses at school. Later, you moved to Salt Lake City and then we saw you less often. It was hard with you so far away but you were able to visit a few times during the summer. On one visit, I took you to UCLA and introduced you to my faculty advisor. She was surprised that I had such a grown-up granddaughter.

We also did fun things during those visits. You loved to ride Suni (Dyane's favorite horse) and play around in the arena. You enjoyed the horses so much that I decided we should have a horseback riding lesson together. You were perfectly calm and completely at ease on your horse but I was nervous and (I admit it) a little scared. But the trainer was good and, before we knew it, she had us trotting around the arena. It was a fun day and the perfect grandmother/granddaughter experience. An interesting tidbit: your horse was named Dotty and many years later your sister, Sarah, had lessons and rode the very same horse!

Since the horseback riding lesson went so well, Dyane and I decided to send you to a week of horse camp. The camp consisted of the grooming and care of horses as well as the various aspects of riding. On the last day, there were a variety of competitive events and you were determined to win a ribbon. And, your determination paid off. I don't remember the event but, sure enough, there you were with your blue ribbon. Dyane was delighted because she was sure this meant you were going to be a great equestrian. However, her excitement was short-lived. Yes, you had a good time and you were pleased with your win, but it was like, "done that, been there." I don't think you were ever on a horse again. Fortunately, we have plenty of pictures of you on horses and we can relive those memories any time we want.

Family is very important to you and memories of family fun also live on in photo after photo. Photos, for example, of big family Thanksgiving dinners in which we all crowded into the studio behind the house in Altadena. And, photos of you and your siblings. When you were very young, you spent a lot of time with Sarah and Vance in La Puente. I'm so glad your relationships continue to grow – yes, with normal sibling squabbles but with a deep-down affection.

Heather, I know life hasn't always been easy for you. The good part is that you're still very young and have a lot of time to change the course and make it better. Don't look at the past – that's gone. Make plans for the future and decide how you're going to get there. Don't limit yourself. Don't think small. It's a big world and there are countless opportunities. You just have to be open to them.

XVIII

LETTER TO ANDREW

February 21, 2012

Andrew, I'm writing this letter to you on your 27th birthday to share with you my memories of your birth and early childhood. When Vincent told me that your mom, Cecilia, was pregnant, I assured him I would do all the right things by all of you but first he had to give me time to be sad. Your dad was not yet 21 and I was sad that you would be born to two very young parents who had no real goals for the future or any idea what it would take to raise a child. You deserved better than that. My only consolation was that, from the beginning, your parents understood they needed to have you and raise you together – and they both loved you very much.

Things may have been stormy before you were born but your mom and dad attended Lamaze classes together and prepared for your birth as best they could. When your mom went into labor, I didn't see your dad for two days. He was with your mother during the labor and delivery and beyond. Your mom developed a fever after you were born and she needed to be isolated from you until it was resolved. With the doctor's permission, your dad took up residency in an empty hospital room and provided sole care for you for 24 hours. We didn't know much about the importance of bonding in those days, but there is no question that the bond formed between the two of you in those initial hours of life laid the foundation for the relationship you continue to enjoy.

When he arrived home from the hospital, your dad was exhausted and unkempt, but he was happy – he had a son. He took to your mom's house the rocking chair that I had rocked your dad and his siblings in so that your mom could rock you. I believe he also took the cradle your grandpa had made for our kids so that you could continue the tradition. And, he vowed to be an active and involved father.

You cried a lot as a baby – a lot. Your poor mom spent many frantic hours trying to figure out what the problem was and what she could do to pacify you. There were many trips to the doctor, sure there was something terribly wrong. I prayed for healing, your dad sprinkled holy water around your room, and your mom worried over you but eventually you calmed down and things got easier.

Your dad brought you to our house often and the whole family got to enjoy you. You were a beautiful baby and it was a joy to have you around. When you were at our house, your dad took complete care of you. To his credit, he never once asked me to take over or assumed that I was there to watch you. Once, you made a big poopy mess, the kind that runs down your legs. Your dad had you in his room and took your diaper off. Then I watched as he wet a face towel and made countless trips back and forth from you to the bathroom – cleaning you and rinsing off that little towel over and over again. He never complained and he didn't ask for help. You were his son and he did what he had to do.

Your dad attended junior college part time when you were little and he often took you to class with him. He'd describe how you sat on the floor or played quietly at his feet during class and neither students nor teacher seemed to mind, in fact most people thought it was cute. I remember thinking that a single mom would never get away with that but folks were much more forgiving of a single dad.

But, how could anyone not have wanted you around – you were adorable and cuddly. I loved holding you and sitting you on my lap. I was sad at the thought that soon you would be too old to carry. I knew I had to hold you as much as possible while I still had the chance. Then you started to talk. I loved how you called you dad "da'ee" and I clearly remember a conversation in which your dad was trying to explain to you who your grandfather was. You looked at both of them and then I could see the light going on in your brain as you exclaimed, "ees you da'ee!" (he's your daddy). Maybe you had to have been there, but no matter how old you get, that's a memory I will forever hold fondly.

There are lots of other memories also. As you grew older, you were smart and very articulate. I was amazed at how comfortable you were around adults. Once, when you were about six, I took you to work with me for a few hours. You were in my office when one of the supervisors walked in and I introduced you to him. You looked up from what you were doing, shook his hand and said, "Hi, John" as one adult might say to another. John was clearly impressed and I was very proud.

On that same occasion, we walked to a nearby McDonald's for lunch. We ordered and then I fumbled through my purse and wallet looking for money. I was initially frantic to think that I might not have any and then I found a few dollars tucked away. You could see my embarrassment and whispered to comfort me, "That's okay, Nana, I know you're old." I laughed. And, I wasn't even that old back then!

Dyane also has a favorite story. We were celebrating your birthday and she gave you a birthday card for an eight-year-old. You opened and read it and then you gently pulled her aside and whispered in her ear, "Dyane, I'm really nine." You were so careful not to call attention to it or to offend her. Dyane was dumbfounded by how fast you were growing up and absolutely charmed by how you handled her mistake.

Your parents may have struggled with their relationship but they were both focused on doing what was right for you. One of the best things your mom did was get you out of Happy Homes, a development riddled with drugs, gangs and violence. I cheered when you and she moved to Montclair and later to San Diego County. She wanted a middle-class lifestyle for you and knew it could come with a change of environment and hard work. She raised you as a single mom and ultimately entered the nursing field. It couldn't have been easy for her; she didn't have parents or family to help. Instead, she took your cousin, Dennis, into her home when her sister died.

As for your dad, the initiation he designed for your eleventh birthday was a testament of his love for you. At that time, he was the youth minister of St. John Catholic Church in Encinitas and he had some experience in creating rituals for youth in the parish. He also had a special interest in rites of passage. He planned your initiation mostly to celebrate your emerging adolescence, but also in response to his own pain over perceived inadequacies as a father. The initiation may well be the most innovative and artistic venture he has ever produced. It was a life-changing experience, not only for you but for the three generations of men before you: your father, grandfather, and great-grandfather.

When your dad asked Pops to participate in your initiation, Pops was the most excited I'd seen in a long time. Mom resisted the idea because she worried it would be too much for him (neither of them ever stayed up late at night) but he insisted. He didn't really understand the ritual or the symbolism but he sensed it was important and was thrilled to be a part of it with you. Mom, Pops, Sonia and I stayed in a motel that night. The plan was that your dad would call us when it was time for me to take Pops to San Luis Rey Mission. We decided we'd sleep for a while so Pops would not get too tired. When I went to wake him I found him lying down on the edge of the bed fully clothed (including shoes) so that he would be ready to jump up and leave at a moment's notice.

It was raining that night and I was having trouble seeing street signs so I was going very slowly and probably swerving. Suddenly, there were bright lights behind us and I realized it was a police car. The Officer looked us over and wasn't at all sure about my story that we had to get to the mission. In the end, however, he led us there - no doubt concluding that we were strange but not dangerous. Still, I could see in the rearview mirror that he hung around until your dad came out to greet us.

Pops' experience didn't end that night. He continued talking about your initiation as one talks about highlights in his/her life. He felt a special bond with you – a connection that was unspoken, without boundaries, deep.

Andrew, I want you to live every day to the fullest. Challenge yourself, sacrifice when you must, and plan your future methodically. Be thoughtful about every decision you make and you'll be fine.

Andrew Olea
Initiation 2-21-96 (Ash Wednesday)
San Luis Rey Mission – Oceanside, Ca

Turtle Head Dress – Navaho Native American Tribe symbol of
strength & longevity given to boys at early age.

Ashes – Christian symbol of temporal state of human experience
prompting grief, humiliation and penitence.

Chest Protector – Putting on armor of God representing
Righteousness (Eph. 6:14)
Faith and love (1 Thes. 5:8)
Painting on chest represents all symbols used
in this initiation ceremony.

Crucifix – (around his neck, under the chest protector)
Symbol of true love and power as seen in suffering.

Bible – The living Word of God. Our faith connection to the
stories of our people.

Flashlight – The light that only a father can freely give to his son.
This light cuts through the darkness, leads us towards
manhood and guides us into the arms of God.

127

XIX

LETTER TO SARAH

April 26, 2012

Sarah, I'm writing this letter to you on your 22nd birthday to share with you my memories of your birth and early childhood. When your dad, Michael, and your uncles, Vince and Chris, were teenagers and young adults, we always had young people around – in the house, in the yard, everywhere. When there was a party in the back yard, those numbers could be in the hundreds. Except for a few of the boys' best friends, I didn't pay attention to who they were – just young faces, mostly smiling – with me mostly trying to get away from the noise. Your mom, Kathy, was one of those faces. I don't know how long your mom was one of the gang that frequented the house, but I do remember finding out much later that the "rocker" outfit I wore for Halloween in 1984 was your mom's. Your dad had borrowed a short denim skirt and a leather jacket from a friend so I could have a costume for work. I didn't learn until after your parents were married that I had worn your mother's clothing.

Your dad was eager to participate in your birth because he had missed out on Heather's delivery since she had come so fast. But he missed out on yours also. He told me the story with tears in his eyes. The nurses were routinely monitoring your mom's labor and then suddenly they were franticly rushing her to the operating room. Your heart rate had dropped dangerously low (the umbilical cord probably wrapped around your neck) and your mom needed an emergency caesarian section. Your dad didn't know what the commotion was all about – no one had time to explain it to him. All he knew was that something terrible was happening and he thought he might lose you or your mom, or both.

I got the word on your birth at work and announced it in a meeting I was holding. I rushed to the hospital and there you were, a tiny bundle weighing 4 lbs. 6 oz. I don't remember you requiring any special care and you came home a few days later when your mom was discharged. You were so tiny, though, that nothing fit you. Dyane and I went shopping and bought you preemie diapers and clothing. Someone suggested I buy you doll clothes but I wouldn't have it. It required some searching but we found sufficient clothes to tide you over until you gained a few pounds and could fit into regular baby sizes.

Your first year of life was pretty normal. Your parents rented a house in Covina and were typical doting parents. You were adorable and smart and reached developmental milestones easily. You had a huge first birthday party and I remember thinking it was a shame that you wouldn't remember it later. As it turned out, you slept through most of it anyway.

Vance was born 17 ½ months after you. The first time Dyane and I went to your house to see him, I took you a baby doll so you wouldn't be jealous over the attention we might give to Vance. You loved your baby doll and held her close to you, mimicking your mom as she held and fed Vance. I don't remember you having a problem adjusting to being a big sister. It was hard to imagine you having a problem with anything – you were tough from the start!

When you were a toddler and Vance was a baby, Dyane and I occasionally babysat you, sometimes overnight. Even though I was an experienced mom, I found myself completely overwhelmed at these times. I remember you walking away from me in one direction and Vance crawling away from me in the opposite direction and me in a panic as to who to go after first. And Dyane wasn't much better. She could handle a herd of galloping horses but she met her match with the two of you. When each visit was over, the house looked like it had been hit by a tornado and we felt like we had been run over by a couple of 18-wheelers.

No doubt you also enjoyed those visits, largely because of the horses. As soon as you could sit and balance Dyane got you up on Suni, holding on to both of you. You loved riding him and, as you got older, you liked giving carrots to all the horses - Suni, Fox and Akela. Except for one time, that is. When you were about three, you and Vance were visiting and Dyane had a 50-lb. sack of carrots from which you could feed the horses. But you shook your head and walked away saying, "No, Vance." Then you watched as your baby brother took one carrot after another out of the sack and, without even looking up, handed them back to the grateful horses. From the beginning, you called Suni "Goggie." When it was time to go home, your dad would have to back up the car so you could tearfully say good bye to Goggie.

As cute as you were, you were also mighty stubborn. Before you turned three, Dyane and I were watching you and Vance overnight. It had been a long day and it was getting late. I tried to explain that you would be spending the night with us but you wouldn't have any of it. You were in your playpen and you stood up and said loudly and defiantly, "I'm tired and I'm sleepy and I want to go home – and **you're not listening**!" When I finally stopped laughing I was somehow able to convince you that you would be fine with us.

Right around the same time, I met you and your dad at a coffee shop. Your mom didn't join us but she did ask that your dad take home a piece of pastry for her. As we finished eating you started reminding your dad to order the pastry. He was deep in conversation and not paying that much attention to you. "Dad," you said, "Dad – the pastry." "Dad." "Dad." Finally, you couldn't stand it any longer. With a disgusted look you shouted, "**Never mind, I'll get it myself**" and bolted out of your seat to order the pastry at the front counter.

If you want to see what sheer determination looks like, there's a photo of you hitting a Ninja piñata (it must have been Andrew's birthday). It didn't matter that the piñata was bigger than you or that the stick was bigger than you, the look on your face says it all. You were going to conquer the situation no matter what!

But the ultimate memory of your stubborn determination took place when I took you to Sears to buy you shoes. You couldn't have been more than three years old but already quite fashion-minded. You loved white patent leather shoes with bows – completely impractical for playing in our backyard which consisted of dirt and sand around the horses. I wanted to buy you some sturdy tennis shoes and knew I would have to sell you on the idea. We walked around looking at a huge assortment of shoes but the only ones you would consider were the frilly feminine ones. I found some white and pink tennis shoes that lit up when you walked and begged you to try them on. You refused. I begged you some more, trying not to create a scene in the crowded store. Finally, you agreed to try them on but absolutely insisted that they would not fit you. "I'll show you," you said. As soon as I put the shoes on you, without taking a step or missing a beat, you fell straight forward to the floor as you exclaimed, **"See, I told you!"** We got some odd looks and I quietly bought the tennis shoes as you stood by rolling your eyes. Fortunately for both of us, in time you learned to love those shoes.

Every Easter, the entire extended family came to our house and you loved hunting for Easter eggs. You knew exactly how this traditional activity went: you would delicately carry your Easter basket as you searched in the side garden for brightly colored eggs – always looking delicate and feminine but determined to fill your basket. The Easter photos we have of you are among Dyane's favorites.

We also love the pictures of you at Disneyland. You had fun at the petting zoo but mostly you slept in the Disney stroller. Dyane's niece, Rebekah, was visiting at the time and she and your uncle Chris went with us to help. Rebekah also went with us to the Wildlife Way Station, a zoo-like park that provides refuge to rescued wild animals. You loved animals of all kinds (remember when you wanted to be a veterinarian?) and it was easy to find someplace with animals to delight you.

So, we've established that you were cute, but you were also talented. Your drawings were amazing, with incredible attention to detail. The picture you drew of a family wedding showing the profiles of the people in attendance took our breath away. The wall hanging you made in second grade depicting important events in your life still hangs in our study and the heart you drew with tears streaming down to illustrate your parents' separation is as touching today as it was when you drew it.

I'll never forget that day in March, 1997 when I got a call from a social worker telling me that you and Vance had been taken into protective custody. Your parents were separated at that time and drugs were found in your mom's apartment. Dyane and I had been worried for some time about your welfare and the kind of care you were receiving from your parents, but when things got really bad your grandmother, Cassie, was there to rescue you and you would be okay for the moment. We had dreaded the possibility of this day coming but it was shocking just the same.

The social worker told me that she was releasing you and Vance to Cassie. She had asked you if you had a preference and you told her you did not want to come with me. She said it as though there was something wrong with me, but the reality was that you did not want to change schools. School had been the one constant in your life and the one place where you were able to succeed and you were recognized for your achievements. You knew how far away I lived and could not bear the thought of yet another change in your life. And so you were absolutely adamant that you did not want to live with me.

A court hearing was held three days later. Cassie and I both attended the hearing and Cassie agreed that you and Vance should stay with me. The judge ordered it and everyone seemed satisfied – except you. I promised you that you would not have to change schools but you did not believe me. When I got you home, you were still fuming. Dyane vividly remembers the disgusted look on your face when you walked through the door.

I kept my promise, though. For the rest of that school year, I drove you from Altadena to Murray School in Azusa for your first grade 8:00 a.m. class, drove back home and got Vance ready, drove him to his half day kindergarten class, returned home, then returned to school in the afternoon to pick you both up (you got out at different times so there was a 45 minute period in which we waited for Vance). I spent four hours on the road each day but it was well worth it to watch you excelling in and loving school. You never once complained about getting up at 6:00 a.m. to be on the road at a little past 7:00 or about the many hours we spent on the freeway.

When you came to us, you were definitely a parentified child; that is, you were used to being in charge and acting as the parent in the family. The hardest thing for me was to convince you that I was the grown-up and you were the child. You wanted to call the shots and when you didn't get your way you could fly into a rage, screaming uncontrollably and not letting me get a word in edgewise. Often you ended your tirade with, "And you had five kids!?" meaning how could I have raised five kids and still be so clueless. It took a very long time for you to let go and just enjoy being a child.

One of the first things we did when you came to us was clothes shopping. Remembering my previous experience with the tennis shoes, I decided to do it alone. I left you and Vance in the car with Dyane while I ran into Sears – simple, right? Not so much for Dyane. You had a screaming fit, insisting that I wouldn't know what to buy you. It was impossible to calm you down so Dyane decided to drive up and down Colorado Blvd. trying not to attract attention, but the screaming continued. It occurred to me later that she would have had a hard time explaining to law enforcement how she came to have these two little kids (obviously not happy and obviously not hers) in her possession.

As it turned out, you loved the clothes I bought you. In fact, you couldn't believe I had done such a good job and from then on, you trusted my judgment completely. That was quite something because you took great pride in looking good. There was a full-length mirror in your bedroom and you checked yourself out front and back any time you left the house, even just to play. That could be a problem in the morning when you wanted to try on different outfits until you looked perfect. Eventually we worked out a system by which you would decide on an outfit the night before. That saved both of us.

When Dyane and I saw how delicate, frilly and feminine you were, we called you a "foo foo girl." That is, until we took you hiking. We had many wonderful trails around the house and at first, we only hiked the ones we could walk to from the house. One day we decided to go a bit further although we were worried that it might be too tough for you – it was steep and rocky with a creek running through it. I pictured Dyane having to carry you because you wouldn't want to get wet or dirty. Boy, were we wrong! You ran with abandon, easily jumped from rock to rock, got soaking wet, and thoroughly enjoyed getting filthy. You proved to us that day that you could be a tomboy too – in fact it was clear that you gave 100 percent to everything you did.

You spent 20 months in our home and this was a very difficult time emotionally for all of us, but it was also a time of enormous growth for you. Initially you were angry, defensive, confused, and insecure. For example, right after you came to us, you stayed with Dyane while I ran an errand. You started to cry, telling Dyane that you didn't like being left with strangers. She told you she was not a stranger; she had known you all your life. You calmed down immediately as you realized you could trust her and we were both there to protect you. A year later when I was out of town overnight, Vance came to my room at night and, finding an empty bed, went crying to you. Instead of trying to fix the problem yourself (as you would have done previously) you woke Dyane and turned it over to her. Now you were reacting appropriately – like a child.

That didn't mean you never reverted to acting like a parent. Your dad used to call you every night and his conversations with you were often more like two peers discussing the day's events than a parent talking to his child. I could only hear your side of the conversation but it sometimes included statements like, "Oh, dad, you're so irresponsible!"

As you were working out who was the parent and who was the child, you were also trying to understand your relationship to me and to Dyane. We bought you things and we took you places but you were confused as to what you had a right to and what was extra. It all came to a head after a trip to a children's fair and petting zoo. The outing had turned sour and you and Vance were very unhappy and very vocal on the way home. You said something about what we "owed" you and I knew I had to address your confusion.

That night after dinner, the four of us had a family meeting and I carefully explained that there were some things you had a "right" to, simply by virtue of being children. Some of these were food, clothing, a home to live in, medical attention, an education, and protection from harm. You didn't have to do anything to earn these things – we owed them to you because we were the adults in the home. On the other hand, things like movies, outings, toys, and special treats were not owed you – they were extras. They depended on whether we could afford them, or whether we thought they were good for you, or whether you had earned them.

It was a fairly cerebral discussion and I didn't expect you to fully understand. But you did - completely. At best, I had hoped the talk would make me feel better and maybe create the foundation for a future discussion. But you and Vance really got it. Many later debates were quickly settled by asking whether the issue at hand was a right or a privilege.

Sometimes you gave me credit for more than I deserved. From the beginning, I had always insisted that you and Vance ride in the rear of the car securely buckled into a car seat. There were no laws about it at the time – only recommendations, but I was fierce about it. Years later, we were watching the news on television one evening when a report came on regarding the need for children to ride in the back seat in a car seat. You turned around and said with great disdain (and perhaps the tiniest bit of admiration), "They got it from you, you know!"

I was really glad you were in the back seat of the car one day as we drove home from school. We were on the freeway talking about events of the day as usual. Suddenly and without warning a large metal sign (around 3' x 4') flew out of the back of a truck about three car lengths ahead of us. The sign whipped back and forth in the wind across all freeway lanes and we watched in horror as the sign hit our front windshield, shattering it into small pieces and showering the inside of the car with glass. You completely kept your cool – trusting me and taking your cue from me as to how to react. We made light of it even though I'm sure you were as scared as I was.

During your stay with us, Dyane and I did everything possible to expose you and Vance to a middle-class lifestyle. You didn't know it (you still might not) but your early years were ones of deprivation and neglect. There were times when you didn't know where you were going to sleep that night and other times when you had to wake your parents up to feed you. I knew we had to show you there was another way to live – a way that included going to work every day, paying bills routinely, getting medical and dental care, planning ahead, and making thoughtful decisions.

We didn't know how long you'd be with us but we were determined to make the time count. We filled your bedroom with books and educational toys. We read to you every night for at least 30 minutes. We didn't allow television except for select children's programs and a Friday night movie. We helped you with your homework and attended all your school functions. Most importantly,

136

we provided a structured environment in which you felt secure and safe.

Actually, I think we went a little crazy with our commitment to expose you to the best activities. Dyane became what I called the "activities director" scouring newspapers, magazines, and bulletin boards, and making endless phone calls to find summer camps and weekend activities that would enrich your lives and, of course, be fun (there wasn't much internet surfing at the time). If she had had her way, you and Vance would have gone to Space Camp in Houston – she lobbied hard but I put my foot down. For her, time and money were no obstacles if it was an awesome activity for you.

You attended some pretty spectacular camps during the two summers you spent with us. There was the Arboretum in Arcadia, a beautiful setting for nature-inspired arts and crafts. The camp at the Natural History Museum in LA (near the Coliseum) provided lots of exciting activities and the California Science Center (which opened in February of 1998) focused on interactive science experiments that you and Vance loved. Then there was the Children's Museum in Pasadena which was small but offered a camp with a good combination of learning and fun. We took you to the Pasadena Museum often because it was close to home and was a nice place to spend the afternoon.

Whenever Dyane and I think about the Pasadena Children's Museum, we remember how precocious you were. One afternoon, we were all walking from the museum to the car and suddenly Dyane and I realized you were deep in conversation with an adult woman who was walking next to us. She wasn't talking *to* you like an adult might to a child. She was talking *with* you and clearly enjoying your company. You had a knack for doing that. You'd walk up to a total stranger and say something like, "Oh, I love your earrings," and that would be the start of a heartfelt conversation. And you were only seven!

Most camps lasted about two weeks but the Hollywood Bowl children's program ran for six consecutive Saturdays. You thoroughly enjoyed participating in the music programs that were followed by an arts and crafts session. Pretty much you enjoyed every place we took you: our trip to Bishop for Mule Days where the four of us spent the night in a two-person tent (Dyane tried to sleep in her truck but nearly froze to death); the Wild Animal Park in San Diego where you especially liked feeding the giraffes and the lorakeets; the Gene Autry museum where you spent hours dressing up in wild west outfits reminiscent of *Little House On The Prairie*; the Griffith Park Observatory where Dyane took you to see the stars; and the Monterey Bay Aquarium that we toured with your aunt, Margaret, in San Jose.

We also took you many times to UCLA. We wanted you to feel comfortable in an academic environment and really wanted you to set your educational goals high. Dyane took you alone to a book fair and we took the two of you to walk around campus and to the sculpture garden. My fantasy was that you would apply to graduate school at UCLA and attach to the application photos of you and Vance in the sculpture garden.

Yes, I started thinking about graduate school for you when you were in the second grade. After finishing first grade at Murray School, you agreed to attend Loma Alta School located about a block right behind our house. Fortunately, you loved it there. Of course, you did well academically and made friends easily. You walked to school with Annie who was your age and lived two doors down from us. She and Ashley (who lived on another block) became your best friends. When the school put on a talent show, you organized a group to impersonate the Spice Girls – choreographed songs, scheduled practices, did it all. It was quite impressive.

The one thing you had that your friends didn't was the horses. You liked the horse rides in the backyard so much that we got you private horseback riding lessons and took you to horse camp. The instructor was a lady that Dyane knew to be excellent with children and she had really good staff. You rode Dotty (the same horse Heather had ridden years before) and Vance rode the pony, Magic. You did very well and really enjoyed the experience.

138

You had amazing natural ability. Dyane hoped you'd be inspired to become an equestrian but you seemed to lose interest as you got older.

You didn't disappoint Dyane when it came to appreciation of the arts, however. When you were seven, I bought tickets to the Nutcracker Suite at the Pasadena Civic Auditorium. You wore a beautiful new dress, a fabulous new coat, dressy shoes and lacey stockings. You looked stunning! I decided to stay home with Vance because he wasn't in a good mood. When you got there, you checked out all the other little girls, satisfying yourself that you looked really good. Dyane bought you a souvenir program and rented opera binoculars and you were set. You followed the program attentively and made Dyane proud!

When Dyane and I were planning to move to the Northwest and put the house in Altadena up for sale, I told your therapist, your social worker, and your parents that if you did not return to one of your parents before we moved, I would become your legal guardian and raise you as my own. That November, the court returned you to your mother who lived with Cassie. You and Vance had always understood that your stay with us was temporary and that the goal was reunification with your parents. In February of 1999, I moved up north and Dyane followed in June. It was a new beginning for all of us.

The story of Rosie the turtle deserves special mention. One weekend when you were out with your mother, you and Vance each got a baby turtle, only about 1½ inches long. Vance's turtle had a cracked shell and unfortunately died within about a week. You asked us to keep your turtle even after you returned home because you knew that would give the turtle the best chance of survival. Needless to say, Dyane was up for the challenge. She found a veterinarian that specialized in exotic animals and learned from him that your turtle was a female red-eared slider who needed to eat in water. She got Rosie a large aquarium (approx. 50 gal.) and by the time we moved she was a full-fledged member of the family.

But Rosie was still growing and soon outgrew the aquarium. Dyane researched the subject and then designed and had built a special pond and waterfall in the front yard - four feet deep and with a blue plastic tub in the middle so that Rosie could hide from predators and hibernate over the winter months. You were visiting us when we introduced her to the pond and we had you do the honors. Admittedly we were nervous that first winter when we couldn't see Rosie under the ice – but then spring came and there she was, alive and well. She loved her pond although sometimes she climbed out and roamed around the property, even following Dyane if she had a piece of chicken for her. Once she disappeared for about four months (we were sure she had met her demise) and then decided to come home. Sadly, Rosie didn't survive her third winter, but no one could question the quality of her life while she was with us.

On another visit with us, I decided that you and Vance had to experience flying. When you were little you were terrified of the idea and Vance had such a fear of heights that I didn't know how it would go. The one thing I knew for sure was that I had to go with you. So, for your return trip, the three of us took a flight to Los Angeles. Your dad and Bea picked you up at LAX and I did a turn-around. The experience was better than I could have expected – a wonderful introduction to an activity you continue to enjoy.

The next time we all flew together was after I retired in 2004. You, Vance, Pops (88 years old at the time) and I flew to Maryland to visit Sonia and her husband, Miguel. While there we made several trips to Washington DC, visited all the museums and tourist attractions including the National Zoo, and went sightseeing in Baltimore. You were in your gothic stage at the time and sported black clothing and makeup but you graciously hid your nose piercing so as not to embarrass me. I'll never forget when we were on the grounds in front of the Capitol Building and a young man asked you what college you went to. You smiled and coyly replied, "I'm in junior high school."

Sarah, since you were a toddler you have demonstrated a dogged determination to do things your way and to be in control of your life. I understand the dynamics of your thinking based on your childhood experiences. As a toddler, you (and your family) struggled with what was in front of you – the next meal and where you would spend that night. There was no long-range planning – your next vacation or what you would do for the holidays. You grew up with the idea that you had to make things happen now because there were no guarantees they would ever happen in the future. And that's how you live your life today. You work hard and you play hard. You want wealth, possessions, experiences, adventures – and you want them now. There's nothing wrong with that at all. The trick is finding a balance between the now and the future. That's not an easy course of action but it may possibly be the most important of your life.

XX

LETTER TO VANCE

September 16, 2012

Vance, I'm writing this letter to you on your 21st birthday to share with you my memories of your birth and early childhood. When you were born, you fulfilled your father's dream. No, not because he had a son (he had been ecstatic over the birth of two daughters) but because he was actually in the delivery room when you were born. Heather had come too fast and he missed her birth and Sarah came as an emergency caesarian - but with you the planets were aligned and everything was perfect. At 6 lbs. 3 oz. you were a good size, you were healthy, and you were beautiful.

I have to admit, I wasn't a doting grandmother constantly by your side. In fact, your dad once commented that I wasn't a "normal" grandmother. He wasn't complaining really, he was just observing that I wasn't on the phone or visiting daily. I was working ten-hour days and taking work home every night. But I had no reason to worry. Your parents dropped by the house occasionally so Dyane and I could see you and at times we babysat you and Sarah overnight. You became good friends with Suni and the other horses and animals. Everyone enjoyed you.

When you were about two we picked you up to bring you to our house and for some reason Sarah didn't want to come. You were napping and we weren't sure how you would react when you awoke and found yourself at our place alone. We had no need to worry, however. You woke up on my bed, looked around, broke out into a big smile, and said, "Eat?" as I handed you a little Vienna sausage. You were fine with the world.

As you got older, you developed a regular routine every time you arrived at our house. You'd run into the house as fast as you could, go into your bedroom, and open a drawer where I kept your toys and a few clothes. When you saw that everything was there as you had left it, you took a deep breath and relaxed. You needed stability in your life and having a few belongings always in the same place made you feel secure.

All the animals also helped provide stability. The horses never frightened you even though they must have looked like giants. You liked feeding them carrots and watching Dyane as she put hay out for them and shoveled manure. Pretty soon you knew the routine and wanted to help. And the horses (Suni, Fox and Akela) were so careful with you, making sure they just took the carrot and not a little finger into their mouths. When you drove away after a day's visit you would wave to them and say, "Bye, bye horsies – love you too!"

You also loved Zoe, although she wasn't sure how she felt about you. Zoe was an Australian Shepherd/Rottweiler mix who had never been around small children. You used to throw yourself on top of her as if she was a shag rug and she didn't know what to do. So, she'd just lie there, not moving and hardly breathing, until you were ready to get up. I think you were a bit too much for her because several times we found her huddled in the back bedroom trying to stay out of your sight. Later we got Scout, a German Shepherd mix, from our neighbors. Scout definitely did not like children but I don't think she would have ever hurt you or Sarah. Still, she barked a lot and looked fierce so we were careful when relatives or neighborhood kids were around.

Mama Katz was an alley cat who used to hang around Mom and Pops' neighborhood. We knew about her because she had given birth to a kitten who was run over by a car in front of their house. When you were about two you were at Mom and Pops' house and you called us from the back door. You were holding Mama with your arms under her two front legs and her two back legs were stretched out with her feet tiptoeing on the ground. She was completely mellow as you yelled, "I like **this** one – she's **big**!"

A little later, Mama gave birth to a litter in Mom and Pops' garage. Pops watched over them and when they were older he moved them to the back yard and cared for them. One day he accidentally closed the shed door on one of the kittens and Mama attacked him and fiercely scratched his legs through his jeans. Mom panicked and Pops asked me to pick up Mama and the kittens and take them to the animal shelter but, of course, they ended up at our house. We kept Mama and one of the kittens, Rascal, and gave the other two kittens away – one to our neighbors who, unfortunately, didn't spay her so, in no time, Mama was a grand-mama. As I was getting ready to send you this letter, Mama died. She was almost 20 years old and was the last of our original animals to pass away.

I don't know if you remember the rabbits, Oscar and Samantha. I hope you do because you loved them. Oscar belonged to your Uncle Frank and Linda and, when they could no longer provide for him, they gave him to us. We bought him a hutch and a large wire cage that we kept in the breezeway of the house and we let him out for short periods to play in the courtyard area behind the house. Then we decided he was lonely so we went to the shelter and picked out a companion for him. Samantha was bigger than Oscar but he fell in love the minute he saw her. She played hard to get but soon gave in and loved him back. They were quite a pair and you enjoyed their antics when they were out in the yard. They really didn't care much for people but they got along well with you.

144

And then there was Papa Gallo. I thought the cock-a-doodle-doo of a rooster would be a nice sound in the morning but Papa Gallo turned out to be a mean rooster who terrorized all of us. Remember how hard it was to get to the back gate so you could walk to school in the morning? I would use a tree branch or something like that to keep him away so you and Sarah could run to the gate. One day you came crying to me that Papa Gallo had gotten you. I asked you where (meaning what part of your body) and you said, "He got me with his talons." I didn't even know you knew the word "talon."

From the beginning, it was clear that you were very smart. We said it to you often (and still do) but you never really believed us. You may have thought we were just trying to make you feel good. But your kind of intelligence is rare. You didn't just memorize information or remember things in little compartments to be spit out later. You understood concepts, how they relate to one another, and how they lead to new ideas. You have a curious, creative mind.

Of course, your curiosity did get you in trouble sometimes. Or, maybe it was just plain mischief. When you were a toddler we took you and Sarah to Disneyland. You were too young for rides but you really enjoyed the petting zoo. However, the animals were never the same again after you were there. There was an old goat that you and Sarah petted gently; then when no one was looking you took a flying leap and landed on his back a la Gene Autry or Roy Rogers. Boy, the look of surprise on that goat's face. And then the look of horror when you crept up behind him and had your finger ready to poke his butt. I think he would have died of embarrassment but I snatched you just in time!

On your third birthday, you demonstrated another part of you – your extreme sensitivity. Your dad threw you a big party at the condo where he was living. It was a huge affair and everyone from both sides of the family as well as friends attended. You were overwhelmed and very unhappy throughout most of it because your parents had just separated. You acted as though your heart was breaking and it was very sad for all of us.

A year later, you had a birthday party at your grandma Cassie's house. Someone gave you a present that needed to be assembled. You wouldn't let anyone put it together for you – you had to do it yourself. You started throwing packaging and wrapping around shouting frantically, **"Where's the map, where's the map!"** I had no idea what you were talking about. It wasn't until you found the instructions and calmed down that I realized they were the "map" you were looking for. You looked at the instructions for less than 15 seconds, put them aside, and assembled your toy perfectly. The rest of us looked at one another in utter amazement.

You were in kindergarten when you were taken into protective custody because of drug use by your parents. At the first court hearing, you were running all over the courthouse and your attorney had to interview you as you hid under a bench. Sarah was very upset by the whole process but you seemed resigned to your new home with me and Dyane. During the 20 months you lived with us, we created many memories – some good, some sad, and some funny.

Mostly I remember how smart you were. One summer morning you were sitting at the kitchen table and you picked up a grapefruit. You looked at it for a while and then said, "Hmmm, it takes up space and it has weight, so it must be matter." We knew you learned this at one of the camps you attended, but the point was – you really got it!

Dyane and I did our best to create a happy environment for you in your bedroom. We filled it with books, toys and educational material. When Sarah was learning to read, sometimes her homework was to read the same chapter of a book every night for a week. While she read, you played quietly on the floor, not appearing to be paying any attention. But if she stumbled or hesitated on a word, you immediately piped up with the correct word. You were not only listening, you had memorized the passage.

Dyane was excellent at finding exciting and challenging camps, museums and other activities for you and Sarah.

Occasionally, she would take you by herself because I was working on a school project. On one particular Saturday, she took you to NASA's Jet Propulsion Laboratory (JPL) in Pasadena for a kid's interactive fair, including an exhibition of the Martian Rover. Your dad was visiting that day, so the three of you went and Sarah stayed with me.

Most of the children at the fair were sons and daughters of JPL engineers. There was a long line to see the Rover and you were anxious to get to the front of the line but you waited patiently. They allowed each child to go up individually and take a closer look and most kids glanced at it and then continued on to other venues, like face painting. Not you, however. You were fascinated by the space vehicle and studied it from every angle, including underneath. You were truly trying to figure out how it worked and you took your time. The JPL officials did not rush you or move you along. They were probably pleased to see a kid who was actually curious about space. As for Dyane, she couldn't have been more proud of you.

While you were with us, Dyane and I made books and reading a priority for you. You had library cards at both the local Altadena library and the Pasadena library. We also took trips to book stores like Vroman's and Barnes & Noble. One afternoon, we took you and Sarah to a bookstore and told you each to pick one book to buy. You impatiently ran through the children's section picking up several books but not showing particular interest in any one. Instead, you spent most of the time running around and playing. When we were ready to go home I asked you which book you wanted to buy. You said, "The body book!" and ran around franticly looking at all the discarded books. You found it – a book that described and illustrated the various systems of the human body. You loved that book and were fascinated by how the body worked. You especially liked pictures of the ear canal and descriptions of how urine was formed.

You also enjoyed the many videos we bought you, such as the *National Geographic Really Wild Animals* series and the *Eyewitness* series on scientific topics. Since we didn't allow television, we also acquired an array of entertaining films suitable for children. Sarah loved typical chic flicks like *Sound of Music* and *Little Women*. You liked animal stories from *Andre* to *Black Stallion*. But your favorite film was *Searching for Bobby Fischer*, a story based on the life of a child prodigy chess player. You didn't tire of watching that movie.

One of my favorite memories of how bright you were is when I was trying to get you to complete a page of math problems. "Just get it over with," I begged. You were angry and you absolutely refused to sit still and I finally said you were not moving until the page was finished. You bellowed "**Okay!**" in a disgusted tone and grabbed the pencil out of my hand. Then you worked each problem swiftly, hardly taking a breath between them and certainly without struggling or using your fingers. I was following behind you to correct you and, honestly, *I could not keep up with you.* You were done in a few minutes and there were no errors on the page.

Yes, you were impatient – but you were also wonderfully curious. When we bought you a little wooden camel that was carved to show a baby inside you studied it with great fascination. "How did they *do* that?" you asked as though you were trying to unravel a great mystery. We couldn't answer your question but we were pleased by the degree of your inquisitiveness.

We weren't the only ones privy to your curiosity. One day I took you to a local shoe repair place to pick up some boots Dyane had dropped off. The repair man was a gruff-looking old guy. As I was talking with him, you (as you often did) snuck into the work area behind the counter. My heart stopped as I ran to grab you before he did. But then you started asking him questions: how did this work; what was that for; can I see that. The man changed before my eyes as he answered your questions and showed you his wares. I think no one had ever shown such an interest in his work and he was absolutely charmed. Your curiosity was genuine and he knew it. You made his day.

We had a similar experience when I took you for an eye exam. They sat you behind a large machine with lots of moving

148

parts and I was nervous about how you would react. Then the questions started: what is this and what does it do and how does it work. The optometrist was delighted to answer your questions and demonstrate the various parts of the machine. But you didn't stop there. You followed the technician into the back room and before I could find you she was giving you a tour of the room and explaining why they kept the batteries in the refrigerator. The optical staff loved you and their eyes would light up when we walked in for subsequent appointments.

You did seem to have a way with technicians. When you needed some blood drawn, the lab technician was ready to mechanically poke you in the arm and move on. But you stopped her and asked her to explain what she was going to do and how she was going to do it. She was hesitant at first but then decided it was a reasonable request. You listened intently and then put out your arm and watched with detached fascination as a couple of vials were filled with blood. You were so excited that you then sat next to Sarah as she had her blood drawn and talked her through the process (she didn't watch but then I never do either).

The dentist may not have been outwardly charmed, but he understood you and I think he appreciated you. You had some cavities that needed to be filled but you were afraid of the needle and the dental equipment. There could have been a terrible scene but the dentist didn't rush you and instead suggested that you watch him work on another child. You looked on as the child got the numbing shot and you could see that the dental work didn't hurt. You agreed to a return appointment and, as you promised, you sat quietly and had your cavities filled. No fuss – smart dentist – smart Vance.

Not all activities were of the no-fuss variety, however. When Dyane and I took you and Sarah to a Hollywood Bowl children's program, you decided to participate in your own way. The program consisted of a music session followed by arts and crafts. You weren't particularly eager to sit quietly through a music program, even though it was child-oriented and interactive. So instead of sitting, you spent the time going up and down the escalators with me following close behind. At first I tried to contain you but I soon learned it was easier just to let you go as long as you weren't hurting anything and I was close enough behind to see you. You certainly didn't act as though you were a Hollywood Bowl fan but when the program ended you asked with great enthusiasm whether we were going to return the following year.

We chose not to return to the Hollywood Bowl the following year. But when we enrolled you and Sarah in a Yamaha Music program, we were not given a choice. The Yamaha program was a creative and highly successful method of introducing children to music and musical instruments. It was a small class of excited children and parents and a very enthusiastic instructor. But you were not into listening. You wanted to walk around and pound on the keyboard at will. When you decided to play one of the large pianos in the room, Dyane took you out of the room with you kicking and screaming. Needless to say, the instructor (not so delicately) asked us not to return.

At the Gene Autry Museum, you ran out (literally) on your own – again with me in hot pursuit. I had tried to interest you in the various displays and activities but you weren't much interested. When we got to the exit, you took off in a sprint heading to a busy intersection. Terrified, I ran after you and thanked God that my 57-year-old legs didn't fail me. As usual, you had no idea what the problem was or why I could possibly be upset.

While at the Gene Autry museum your fear of heights became evident. I was not prepared when you froze at the top of a wide staircase. Slowly, you inched your way backwards until you were leaning against a back wall. I didn't think we would be able to move you but somehow we got you in an elevator and you were fine. That wasn't our first experience with heights. Once, while playing in a park, you climbed up a pole structure that was supposed to resemble a fort. You got up okay but then you turned around and looked down. You were completely immobilized and I (also afraid of heights) had to go up and practically carry you down.

150

There were many times when we planned good times for you and you gave back, shall we say, some tense moments. When we took you to Mule Days in Bishop, we anticipated a camping experience and some entertaining mule shows. You were not okay when you learned that camp fires were not allowed and you would not be able to roast marshmallows. It just wasn't the same to roast marshmallows and make 'smores' on a camping stove but we tried.

The mule shows were wonderful and Sarah and Dyane enjoyed them from the bleachers. You and I, however, spent our time *under* the bleachers – mostly me chasing after you. You were sweet as you petted the mules in their stalls, but your sweetness came and went. On one occasion, you ran into an open area where there was a line of porta-potties and a long line of people waiting to use them. You ran up to one of the potties, threw open the door, came face-to-face with a very surprised user, slammed the door closed, and continued running. All this time I'm praying nobody knows you belong to me!

That was not the only time I prayed that nobody knew you were mine. When we took you to the Wild Animal Park in San Diego some innocuous remark Dyane made about us sticking together ticked you off as we entered the park and you were in a bad mood all day. As we watched an elephant show, you ran up and down the bleachers and park officials posted people at each end of the stadium to make sure you didn't jump into the elephant arena or get into other mischief. They also kept track of you as we navigated the park and, if I lost you for a minute I would hear, "Hey, lady, he's over here!" I think I held my breath during the entire outing, not knowing what would happen next.

Horseback riding lessons and summer horse camp proved to be a mixed bag, but I must say, mostly a good one. You loved Magic the pony and looked forward to riding and grooming him. You were so little that the tiny pony towered over you, but you were a natural rider and always looked very comfortable in the saddle.

I will forever be grateful to your first-grade teacher, Mrs. Syzonenko. I volunteered as a teacher's aide in your classroom two days a week so I know firsthand that she was an extremely competent teacher and compassionate person (aka a saint). She never fussed at you nor was she impatient with you even though you did your own thing in the classroom with complete disregard to what everyone else was doing. There was no question there was learning going on in your head but your behavior was contrary and disruptive. Still, she said she enjoyed you and I believe she did. Your special education teacher who worked with you one-on-one also seemed to enjoy you.

One morning, you ran off towards the mountains instead of walking with me to school. You often ran off but usually in public areas, not from home. You went up a slope and refused to come down. I called the principal to let her know what was happening and she suggested I give you an hour and if you weren't down by then to call the Sheriff's Department. Before the hour was up, you came down on your own. Then the emotional floodgates opened and your anger spilled over – anger at your parents, anger at yourself, anger at the world.

All the way to school you ranted and agonized about how everything was your fault – that your parents got in trouble; that you needed to go to court; that you couldn't live with your dad; that everyone was unhappy. You were inconsolable and I wondered what would happen when we got to the classroom. But, once again, Mrs. Syzonenko came through in her usual unruffled manner. She sat the children on the floor around her and allowed you to express your feelings. Then she engaged the children in a discussion around those feelings in a spontaneous and amazing session on why drugs are bad and why parents and grownups are the responsible ones. The children knew instinctively that you needed their caring and support. You calmed down and the class continued.

Your therapist was Linda Bortel, Ph.D. and she saw you and Sarah weekly. She found that you were most receptive to a conversation with her when the two of you were throwing a ball around outside or playing a game like *Battleship*. I don't know how

152

much you opened up to her but she seemed to know everything that was going on. Once, you told her that Dyane had locked you in your room. Dr. Bortel could easily have formed a quick judgment but she calmly asked you questions about the incident. You explained that you were yelling and kicking at the door at the time. You also agreed that if you had stopped the yelling and kicking, she would have let you out. In the end it was clear that you were simply telling a factual story and not trying to get Dyane into any trouble.

Dr. Bortel and I talked about medication for you to make your behavior more manageable. She left the final decision to me but pointed out that medication might dull that bright, curious, quick spark of yours that both she and I loved. In the end, we didn't do the meds, in large part because I didn't want you to grow up thinking that pills were the answer to life's problems.

Fortunately, life isn't always a problem and I remember plenty of happy moments. Every Sunday, I made waffles for breakfast and you loved helping me. With a big grin on your face, you'd run to the bathroom for the little wooden stepstool that helped you reach the counter. Then you'd measure the milk and sometimes crack the eggs that went into the batter. Sarah always sat at the table waiting to be served but you wanted to be in on the action. I still think of you every time I make waffles with the same old waffle iron.

And then there was your magnificent voice. Actually, you had two voices – your indoor voice that was *quiet and sweet* and your outdoor voice that was **loud and deep**. When you were playing inside you had no problem using your *indoor voice.* But when I asked you to call Sarah from outside you complied with your **outdoor voice**. It was startling to hear such a bellow coming out of such a little boy.

You definitely used your outdoor voice when you sang *I believe I can fly* as you walked across the acre of our property. You had a magnificent voice and could be heard down the block. In fact, Annie's mother (who lived two houses down from us) once remarked how much she enjoyed listening to you sing.

Unfortunately, you didn't like to perform in front of people so the world missed out on your beautiful voice.

I think the happiest time of the day for you was when Dyane and I read to you and Sarah before bedtime. We had a huge stack of books and could easily go through two to four books a night. You were consistently calm and relaxed at this time and the only displeasure you ever voiced was that we didn't read one more story. We are so pleased that to this day you continue to enjoy reading books and that Barnes & Noble has become your friend.

Here are just a few of the other good times you had. On Christmas you got so many gifts you actually complained that you were tired of opening them. Every year we had a neighborhood block party and you, Sarah and neighbor Cary got to ride on a fire engine. You quickly mastered the art of roller skating while looking good in full safety attire. You loved playing in the yard – dangling upside down on the monkey bar, climbing the jungle gym, romping in the sprinkler in the courtyard.

In November, two months after you turned seven, you and Sarah were able to return home to your mom and visit regularly with your dad. You were happy for the court experience to be over. The day I drove you to your grandma's house was one of mixed emotions for all of us – relief, joy, emptiness, hope.

Years later, when you and Sarah and I visited Sonia and Miguel in Maryland, you experienced the Capital, the Smithsonian museums, and the National Zoo. But perhaps the highlight of the trip for you was the flying lesson you took from Miguel. He showed you how to inspect the plane before takeoff and then took you up in the air. You did very well until you went back up with Miguel and an instructor in the front seats and you at the rear. You must have had motion sickness because you came back looking a little green.

Vance, you suffered from negative experiences early in your childhood through no fault of your own. But you survived childhood and you're not a kid anymore. You're in charge now – of your present and your future. I know it feels scary; there are so many unknowns. The best advice I can give you is to take one small step

154

at a time. Make plans – do it in writing. What do you want life to look like in one year? What do you have to do to make that happen? I'm not asking you to dream and wish. I'm asking you to plan and do. And, I'm asking you to believe in yourself, because I believe in you.

XXI

RELIGION AND FAITH

I'm a Roman Catholic because I was born and raised one. I grew up in a tightly knit parish community and my family loved all parish activities. Some of my fondest memories are walking to weekday Mass with my grandmother during the summer months; enjoying *tamales* and *champurrado* in the church hall after Sunday Mass; and feeling about the annual church *jamaicas* the way kids today feel about going to Disneyland. I attended parochial grammar school, an all-girls Catholic high school, and an all-women Catholic college.

Why I stay a Catholic is the more important question and the answer is, as they say, complicated. In fact, if I had been raised without a specific religion and were making that decision today, I wouldn't choose Catholicism. I'd more likely be a Buddhist – I admire the notion of mindfulness and the Buddhist search for inner peace. Or, I would be happy as a Quaker, committing my life to peace, non-violence, and the simple things of life. Why would I choose a highly bureaucratic, male dominated, change resistant, often clandestine organization?

I didn't always feel this way. As a child, I wanted to be a saint and admired those who had been martyred for their faith. As a teenager, I wanted to become a nun. In my 20's and 30's, I struggled to remain true to the strict rules of the church, but in my 40's, I attended daily Mass and for years was active in the Charismatic Renewal. I joined prayer groups and participated in healing services and looked forward to the annual Charismatic Convention in Anaheim. I was sincere in my practice and believed it to be compatible with my increasingly feminist values. I was the happiest I'd ever been and thought I had finally arrived. I was a self-confident, liberal, feminist, professional, Catholic woman.

The road to that place had not been easy. I had five babies in six years, two conceived while practicing rhythm – the "natural" birth control sanctioned by the church. My middle child was born with severe developmental disabilities. I went to work when my youngest was six months old. My marriage was not the "happily ever after" I had dreamed about.

After I had my fifth child, I knew that having another baby immediately would jeopardize my physical and emotional health. Still, I fantasized that a family of eight children would be nice and assumed I'd work only until I got pregnant again. I hoped that would be later rather than sooner - I was only 28 and desperately needed a little space between babies. A co-worker was shocked when I confided I was not on the pill. The pill? I knew Pope Paul VI had banned it in his 1968 encyclical, *Humanae Vitae.* I also knew women all over the world were delighted with their newfound ability to control their reproductive health. I pictured a life in which you didn't have to check the calendar to see if you might be ovulating and should avoid sex (assuming your husband agreed) and didn't live in monthly fear of another pregnancy. I decided to see my doctor.

I was on the pill for a couple of years and certainly enjoyed the benefits, but I must have also worried about the moral consequences because I decided to mention it to a priest in confession. I thought he would surely reassure me that I wasn't going to hell when he heard the circumstances of my life and my short-term plan for the pill. Instead, he refused to give me absolution and I left the confessional in tears, much to my embarrassment and to the shock of the people in line outside the confessional booth.

That experience, still vivid today, did not prompt me to go off the pill. It did prompt me to examine my own conscience hoping to align my beliefs to what I imagined was the will of God (not the men who compose the Catholic hierarchy). I could not believe that a benevolent God wanted women to have a stream of babies regardless of their physical and emotional health; regardless of their ability to care for them; regardless of the circumstances surrounding the conception. We may want to believe that all babies are conceived out of pure, marital love but the reality is that many are conceived in a moment of thoughtless passion, in a drunken stupor, even in an act of violence (including rape on the marital bed).

The reasons given by the Church for opposing birth control did not convince me – in fact, they offended me. Contraception is against the order of nature, they say. This means that every act of sexual intercourse must be allowed the potential to result in a pregnancy. I agree that might be natural, but it's not rational. Men and women, because they are rational human beings, are expected to control the many factors that affect all of their bodily systems: cardiovascular, digestive, renal, muscular, etc. We work hard at eating properly and exercising and getting restorative sleep so these systems can perform at an optimal level. We rely on research findings and take advantage of technological advances to improve the quality of our lives. Shouldn't the reproductive system receive equal attention and consideration? Is the fact that the reproductive system is thought of as a "female" system influencing the church's perspective?

Another irrational church teaching is that God told Adam and Eve to "be fertile and multiply;" therefore couples to this day cannot plan the size and timing of their families. I can't believe that a fairly innocuous statement in Genesis was meant to deprive couples of decision-making in the most important expression of their union. It seems to me that Adam and Eve did pretty well for themselves in terms of progeny and perhaps we should be doing more to take care of the children already on earth.

I should not have been surprised by the church's teaching regarding contraception or by my reaction to it. In college, the liberal arts curriculum included a number of theology classes. We had a textbook devoted to the Sacraments and, amazingly, the chapter covering the Sacrament of Matrimony did not once include the word "love." I remember intently looking for some mention of affection, love, sex, attachment – anything that would denote a special relationship between two people. It wasn't there. Marriage was a contract, plain and simple. That was more than 50 years ago, and I'm sure marriage is defined differently in religion classes today. But I'm not sure the message has changed that much.

When post-Vatican II discussions regarding family planning included married couples, I was delighted that women were going to participate in the discourse. Then I realized these couples were selected because they were already completely committed to the historical teachings of the church, claiming that their love was strengthened by the periods of abstinence required by "natural" methods of birth control (about 10 days a month to be truly safe). These couples may have represented Catholic beliefs but they didn't represent any married couples I knew.

To be fair, things seemed to have lightened up in the last 20-25 years. The church's teaching did not change but the subject of birth control appeared to have been put on a back burner. Priests didn't rail over it in Sunday sermons or threaten couples with mortal sin and hell. While they didn't openly counsel couples to form their own conscience, they spoke volumes by simply not addressing the issue at all.

All that changed in January of 2012 when the U.S. Department of Health and Human Services announced that Catholic employers would be required to offer all their employees the full spectrum of family planning services. The Catholic outcry was immediate and furious. Catholic Bishops condemned the ruling as an assault on religious liberty. I couldn't believe it - suddenly we were back in the 50's, only this time with concentrated attention by all forms of media. The Catholic ban on contraception and sterilization became the hot topic on everyone's lips and keyboard. When our local Bishop sent a letter to his parishes urging strong opposition to the federal ruling, I knew I had to take a stance. Here is a portion of the letter I addressed to him on February 12, 2012:

In your letter, you use the word "forced" in italics for emphasis and refer to the "severe assault" on religious liberty. Not only are these words highly inflammatory, but they are not consistent with the facts. (Many) faith based institutions... are already required to provide family planning services to their employees and....nobody has felt forced to do anything: employees of all faiths and religious persuasions have simply been able to access comprehensive health care according to their personal beliefs and conscience. The private decisions made by a non-Catholic woman with her doctor do not in any way impact the private decisions made by a Catholic woman with her doctor.

I agree that religious liberty is a fundamental freedom but I fail to see how allowing my Jewish or Muslim or Buddhist or Methodist neighbors to abide by the dictates of their conscience infringes on my religious liberty. On the contrary, forcing an institution to deny employees the health benefits of their choice infringes on the liberties of those employees. Didn't Jesus Christ teach us by example to be compassionate and non-judgmental?

The Bishops had a lot of support on the issue of health care insurance from the Religious Right because they were united on the subject of abortion. Fundamentalist Christians and Catholic hierarchy raised their collective pro-life voices. Still, only Catholics deny women the right to protect themselves from an unwanted pregnancy (and possibly avoid having to make a more difficult decision later).

I've struggled with my thoughts on abortion over the years. Fundamentally, I believe that life begins at conception. I believe this because everything required to produce a new human being is present from that moment on. If I believe this is when life begins, then I have to believe that abortion is the taking of a life.

Not everyone agrees with this basic premise. Some believe there is a period following conception in which cells are multiplying but there is not yet a soul to make those cells human. Others believe that, until the fetus is viable, a woman should be able to control what's happening within her reproductive system, just as she has control over her other bodily functions. If these are conclusions of conscience, I respect them.

We all make difficult decisions every day based on our fundamental beliefs and other circumstances within our lives, including our state of mind. These decisions and their consequences can only be judged by God who, by the way, is far more merciful and just than we are. Women who have had or are considering an abortion are often fair game for judgment and condemnation. They are talked about as though abortions are an easy answer to promiscuity – how unfair! Who am I to know or understand the physical and emotional factors a woman has to consider in making this decision.

One of my objections to extreme pro-life and pro-choice movements is that neither sees the big picture. Pro-life advocates often discount the needs of the mother and have saving the baby as their only goal. Thus, they justify using intimidating tactics with women considering abortion. Pro-choice advocates often proceed as though there is only one life to consider and the potential baby is of no consequence. They only provide women with a medical procedure. Neither faction offers women the full range of options in a compassionate environment.

I'll just say it upfront. I do not want Roe v. Wade overturned. I want abortion to remain legal. Roe v. Wade does not proclaim abortion as moral or desirable. It simply says that abortion is not against the law. Just because something is legal, doesn't mean I'm obligated to choose it. Adultery is legal but couples don't use its legality as an excuse to commit it. Cigarettes are legal but I choose not to smoke them. Laws do not dictate my moral behavior, my conscience does.   Abortions have been taking place since the beginning of time and they will continue whether they are legal or not. The difference is that if not legal, many women will be at risk of grave injury or death.   When looking at the situation through a non-judgmental lens, I believe it is more moral to protect a woman's health and safety than it is to deliberately put her at risk. When a woman chooses to terminate an unwanted pregnancy, it is not the fault of Roe v. Wade.   Roe v. Wade simply keeps her and her physician from going to jail.

Actually, I consider myself completely pro-life. This means I am against war, against capital punishment, against planned assassinations to protect our country. I value all life, not just the unborn.   I don't understand how some people fight to change abortion laws while they remain unmoved when men, women and children are killed violently in war, vote against abolishing the death penalty, and cheer when patriots assassinate identified bad guys. If ending human life is wrong, it's wrong all the way around.

I know the argument against the three examples I give is that they involve an aggressor.   But what about the hundreds of thousands of innocent civilians who have died in recent Middle East wars? And, what about the growing number of death row prisoners who are being exonerated as the result of newly available DNA testing or because their cases were fraught with racial prejudice? And, since when did "Thou shalt not kill" come with a bunch of exceptions?

Getting back to babies, when I was young, there was only one way to conceive a child but modern technology has changed that.   Today, countless couples and single parents are raising wanted, loved children who are the result of artificial insemination, in vitro fertilization, and surrogacy. But the church chooses to be anti-life on this issue, prohibiting the use of these techniques. That's odd because when Sarah (Old Testament) and Elizabeth (New Testament) found themselves childless in their old age, God didn't say "Oh, well." No, He was sympathetic to the yearning in their hearts and gave them each a son (much to Abraham's and

162

Zacharias' shock). Sometimes God performs outright miracles and other times he lets human intelligence lead to miraculous discoveries.

A serious side issue of in vitro fertilization and one to which I've given much thought concerns embryos that are not implanted. The Church teaches that each embryo is a human life and therefore cannot be destroyed. I understand the thought process, since an embryo that forms in the womb demonstrates its humanity from the beginning; sperm fertilizes an egg and nine months later you have a baby, period, without the mother having to do anything. But when the embryo is formed in a petri dish, it does nothing until it attaches to the uterus. It will never grow or develop on its own. Therefore, I believe that embryos formed outside the human body are potential, but not actual, human life. I'm not suggesting that embryos be created haphazardly, but I don't think properly disposing of them should be likened to murder, especially when they are of such benefit to stem cell research.

It's obvious that most of my anger toward the Catholic Church stems from the Church's treatment of women. That is not what Jesus Christ intended. Jesus had women friends; he made them his disciples; he talked to the Samaritan woman at the town well; he kept an adulterous woman from being stoned to death; he healed women of physical illness and comforted them when they grieved; he had them sit at his feet when he preached; he appeared to them first after he rose from the dead.

Yet, two thousand years later, women are still not equal in the eyes of the Church that Jesus Christ established. We are grateful for the liturgical tasks we are allowed to perform: Eucharistic minister, sacristan, altar server (when I was a child this was unheard of). But we are still denied the priesthood and, therefore, barred from participating in the governance of the Church. We are unable to contribute to any dialogue on issues of morality or doctrine or change. In other words, we cannot participate as full members of the church – we are only spectators.

I was hoping for significant change in my lifetime, but that may not be. There's absolutely no reason why we could not be training women for the deaconate right now, tomorrow. Vocations for the priesthood are dwindling and parishes are sharing priests or going without. The church is in crisis and parishes are looking for men to ordain as deacons - married men, divorced men, retired men. Men – not women. What? Women aren't capable of reading the gospel, delivering a homily, baptizing a child, or officiating over a funeral?

It's not that women haven't tried to break the barrier. In the 1960's, the Immaculate Heart of Mary sisters attempted to implement the decrees and spirit of Vatican II but were thwarted at every move by James Francis McIntyre, Cardinal of the Archdiocese of Los Angeles. The sisters disbanded as an order of nuns in protest. In recent years, there have been many examples of groups of Catholic nuns who have spoken up against the harsh dictates of American Bishops only to be ridiculed and dismissed. In the end, it's all about power and control, and two thousand years of power and control are mighty hard to give up.

My anger towards the church turned into rage when the reports of child sexual abuse by priests started coming in. It didn't seem possible at first. Surely, the press is exaggerating, we thought. And then came more and more reports from all over the country of active priest pedophiles and thousands of child victims. Still we rationalized. In any profession, there's going to be a small percentage of child molesters – coaches, boy/girl scout leaders, teachers, etc. But – priests? Priests who turn bread and wine into the body and blood of Christ; priests who have the power to forgive (or not) our sins; priests who threaten us with eternal hell if we have consensual sex with someone to whom we're not married; priests who represent the living Christ on earth; priests who we hold to a higher standard; priests with whom we feel most safe and trust with our children?

Finally, it hit us, as case after case was substantiated and priest after priest admitted the accusations. Speculation and intrigue turned into ugly fact. And that wasn't even the worst of it. Worse were the cover-ups by church hierarchy that continue to the present day. Priests who should have been reported to law enforcement for their criminal activity were quietly moved to unsuspecting new parishes where they could start anew. Bishops later feigned ignorance of the law; ignorance of the dynamics of child sexual abuse. But - ignorance of morality, of justice, of compassion, of common sense?

The reaction of Catholic laity to the sex abuse scandal varied. Some Catholics left the church in disgust. Others buried their heads in the sand and remained unquestioning in their allegiance to the church. Most surprising to me are the Catholics who resent the amount of money the church has been ordered to pay the victims (in essence blaming them) and scoff at new policies regarding the training and fingerprinting of church volunteers. As for me, I fought to keep my rage from boiling over. I was a child welfare professional dedicated to keeping kids safe. I felt betrayed by my church. I was afraid if I faced the scandal squarely, I would leave – the church, God, Jesus, all of it. And, I would never come back.

Lest you think church scandals are new issues, let me remind you of the well-documented turbulent history of the Catholic Church. Like most Catholics, I haven't read the volumes dedicated to honest church history, but on a CBS News Sunday Morning program there was a segment on the church that piqued my interest enough that I went to the CBS website to read it. These are the words used to describe the Catholic Church: "corruption....scandal....internal conflict....shame....mess.... bureaucratic jealousies....financial corruption....sense of isolation from the real world." I was struck by the truth and I was embarrassed.

The only way I have been able to reconcile my feelings is to separate institutional church from faith. It was the institution, the bureaucracy, the male hierarchy that failed – not the teachings of Jesus Christ. Church is not a place or a person. Church is community in which people love their neighbors. Truly love – the

165

way Jesus did. My reconciliation didn't come overnight. It's still a work in progress. But I do find more peace within myself. I feel no allegiance to the Vatican or to my Diocese. I do ask myself always, "What would Jesus do"?

Since I've already bared my soul on sensitive issues, let me just lay out some of my beliefs in other areas.

Evolution is no longer a theory; it is scientific fact. It is not contradictory to believe in evolution and in the creation of man by God or other Supreme Being. There is a strong possibility that other planets in the universe (or universes) contain life, which may or may not be similar to ours.

The Bible was never meant to be a history or a science book. The Old Testament was written over a long period of time (beginning as early as 1200 B.C.) by many authors, some anonymous. They may have been inspired by God, but He didn't dictate the language. The New Testament was written between about 50-120 A.D. Authors of the bible expressed themselves according to the culture of their day. Their words told stories that were meant to inspire us and act as lessons on how we should live our lives.

I don't believe that homosexuality is learned or a matter of choice. I believe there is incontrovertible evidence that it is the result of nature influenced by nurture. I believe we are born on a continuum that has complete homosexuality on one end and complete heterosexuality on the other. We have no choice as to where on the continuum we fall; it's part of our genetic makeup. But environment, life circumstances and opportunity can play a role and move a person on the continuum. That's why some heterosexuals are more (or less) inclined to form homosexual relationships when they are segregated from the opposite sex (e.g. boarding school, prison). If there's one quality Jesus Christ exemplified it was acceptance. He taught love and inclusion but, unfortunately, many Christians today feel free to defile a large portion of our population. I'm embarrassed by their ignorance.

166

I do not believe Catholicism is the one true church. To believe that would be to negate the billions of people who lived on earth prior to Jesus Christ and the millions who live today outside of Christianity. Only about 17% of the world population is Catholic. How presumptuous it would be to tell the other 83% that their religion or belief system is not valid!

I have known three true atheists in my life – not fallen-away Christians, not agnostics, not angry anti-God crusaders – but true non-believers. These friends have been an inspiration to me because of the way they have lived their lives. They truly cared about people and exemplified Christian values far better than many Christians I know.

In the end, we will be judged by whether we have loved our neighbor. Not by how well we quote the Bible; not by the religion we choose to practice; not by our sexual orientation; not by our immigration status; not by our wealth or poverty; not by our addictions or desires. We will be judged on whether we loved others as we love ourselves; whether we were accepting, tolerant, non-judgmental, giving, gentle, kind.

Now back to the original question: why do I stay a Catholic? It's hard to explain, even hard for me to understand. My faith is an integral part of me – like my love of mountains and the ocean, my need for things to be orderly, my discomfort in social situations. These are more than descriptions of me; they are basic components that make me who I am. My faith is not only in my head; it's in my heart and soul. It nurtures me; it comforts me; it makes me happy. I am emotionally moved by Catholic ritual, sometimes to the point of tears. My reaction is as automatic as flinching when I'm startled by a loud noise and turning away when I'm being poked by a needle. I can't help it.

What do I say to my descendants? I say, look within your heart and soul for what makes sense to you. Don't be spoon-fed; think for yourselves. Explore and question and challenge. If you don't believe, let it be out of conviction and not out of laziness. If you do believe, let it become a part of you.

167

And so - I will continue to be a practicing Catholic, loyal to my God, my local church, my fellow parishioners. But I don't do it because I have to, or even because it's right. I do it because it is who I am.

XXII

STEPHANIE

If you have a child with a serious disability, you already know what I'm going to write because you've lived it. If you don't have a child with a serious disability, you won't fully grasp the complexity and the horror of it all because you don't need to. With a healthy child, your life with that child is defined by a series of joyful milestones that become "remember when…" conversations later. When you learned to walk, started kindergarten, mastered the two-wheel bike, had your heart broken, graduated from high school, landed your first job, got married…. It's no different when you have a child with serious disabilities except the milestones are not joyful. When the symptoms began, the diagnosis, the second opinion, the treatments, the family accommodations, the endless responsibility, the life plan, the guilt….

My first reaction to any hint of a problem with Stephanie was classic denial. I rationalized every symptom, convincing myself they were all positive indicators. She was a remarkably easy baby who cried only occasionally and slept soundly (ignore the high pitched cry followed by deep sleep). She was a beautiful baby who would give me no trouble at all (ignore her lack of interest in eating). When ignoring was no longer an option and the doctor's words penetrated my brain – "seizures....brain damage....wait and see" – the world around me faded. I could see it through the fog and I could respond and react to it but to my core I was consumed with trying to make sense of what was happening.

The one thing I didn't do was ask "why me?" That seemed pointless because...why not me? Why would I think I was so special that bad things couldn't happen to me? I saw sadness and hardship in the world and never thought I should be immune to it. Still, I wanted a reason, some idea why this particular hardship would strike at this particular time. I blamed myself, of course, even when the doctors described Stephanie's condition as an accident of nature at the moment of conception. Not a genetic problem – not caused by something I did or didn't do during my pregnancy – not a birth injury. It doesn't matter because, after a while, the cause is no longer the issue. Guilt takes on a life of its own, unrelenting and cumulative. It is self-flagellation at its finest – if you beat yourself up enough you can atone for whatever you did or didn't do, not only at the beginning, but at every decision-making point throughout her life. I will die wondering what role I played in Stephanie's life and what I could have done to alter the outcome.

The hardest decision I had to make for Stephanie was where she would call home. This isn't the kind of decision that's made once and is done. It's the kind of decision that evolves, slowly and deliberately and painfully, mostly based on circumstances in your face at that moment. When Margaret was born and I couldn't physically care for Stephanie, I had her admitted into Pacific State Hospital for one month (they would have taken her for three). Years later, I agreed to let her stay in the hospital full time until she completed a potty-training program. Years after that, I became hysterical when a social worker described how Stephanie needed structure and consistency that she wasn't getting at home. The social worker was compassionate and reasonable and I listened. During the next few years, I worked with Regional Center on three different placements for Stephanie in the community. When she was 12, I had had enough of out-of-home care and brought her home.

The next four years were trying. Stephanie's unsocialized behavior escalated. She was placed in a school setting for Trainable Mentally Retarded (TMR) children with oppositional behavior. Her tantrums continued – an explosive mix of the terrible two's and teenage rebellion. I could no longer pick her up and carry her off. She weighed more than me and fought back, sounding like a grown woman being assaulted. I turned to Margaret to help me and put an inordinate amount of responsibility on her. I often left her, at age 11 and 12, with the task of getting Stephanie on the school bus (she screaming while bus driver pulled and Margaret pushed). It was either that or my getting to work late, yet again. Margaret was also my primary babysitter when there was no school and I had to work. I regret that I did that to her. I didn't expect much from the boys who were doing normal teenage things. Only one thing was for sure: nothing about our family life was routine or carefree. There were no happy options.

Still, we tried. One Saturday afternoon, I thought I'd treat us all to lunch at a local Bob's Big Boy. Stephanie was in a good mood when we arrived and they seated us at a corner round booth, one that easily accommodated the six of us. Everything went well until Stephanie started to laugh – the kind of laugh that quickly escalated into uncontrollable hysterics. She got louder and increasingly disruptive and then the laughter combined with loud belches and grunts. The kids slid off the booth and went quickly to the car. I did my best to move Stephanie along as we exited the restaurant. There was a family in the booth next to ours celebrating the mom's promotion at work. I apologized profusely as we left for ruining their celebration.

When Stephanie was 16, I knew I had to make some serious decisions about her life – and mine. It was time to dig deep and take an honest look at my options. One of these options was out-of-home placement, with which I already had some experience. I knew it was by no means an ideal situation, but it could provide Stephanie the structure and safe environment she needed. Another option was to reorder my own life, adjusting my work and daily activities so that I could provide her with a permanent home. So that I could be responsible for her – be her physical caregiver – be her mom.

Facts kept running through my head: she was mine; I loved her; nobody could take better care of her than me; taxpayers should not carry her financial burden. Parallel facts ran alongside: our home environment was chaotic for her; I worked full time; I placed too much responsibility on Margaret.

In the end, I chose to find an outside setting for Stephanie. I didn't want a group home supervised by Regional Center – that plan offered little hope of long-term stability. Stephanie had already experienced three of those homes. She was removed from the first home due to neglect reported by me and by her teacher. The second family moved out of town, and the foster mother in the third home suffered a back injury. Instead, I looked for a facility/institution that would remain a constant even as caregivers moved in and out; someplace she could recognize as a permanent home.

I selected Salem Christian Homes in Ontario, California, at that time a large complex with multiple wings, a large activity center, and an ample playground area. I didn't mind the institutional design of the facility; it worked for Stephanie and gave her the structure she needed. Salem has since de-institutionalized and, as of this writing, consists of 19 individual homes housing a total of 111 residents.

Things haven't always run as smoothly as we hoped. At one point, Margaret decided to assume responsibility for Stephanie and moved her to a group home setting in San Jose where she lived. Margaret was ultra attentive to her sister's medical and living needs and quickly burned out. When she moved to the Seattle area, Margaret returned Stephanie to Salem, a good move for everyone.

When I moved to the Pacific Northwest, there were a few years when there was no one available to take Stephanie on holidays. I had no place to keep her safely overnight so all I could do was take her to lunch and the local park on the few occasions that I visited Southern California. The guilt ate at my heart and it didn't help that staff at her home were constantly reminding me that Stephanie really wanted to go home ("suitcase?") for a visit. I felt helpless and could only hope that things would change in the future.

And change they did. Some years ago, Christopher and a girlfriend were able to take Stephanie to their house for some holidays. Now, Michael and his wife, Bea, regularly take her for holidays and special events. Stephanie loves these visits and looks forward to them. I do too because, on occasion, she and I stay at Michael and Bea's house at the same time and, for a night or two, we're a family.

There's no getting around it. I'm still haunted by my failure to keep Stephanie at home, with family. I didn't take care of her. Isn't that what family does? I see other parents who have been able to achieve this with grace. Parents who have children with severe congenital or debilitating conditions, disabled by accident or war, for some reason requiring 24-hour care. Parents who have dedicated their lives to creating safe and loving environments for their disabled children, simply because they are their children and they love them. Parents who sacrificed their personal lives so that they are now defined by the one act of taking care of their child. I admire and envy these parents.

When I made a life plan for Stephanie outside her home, I didn't know what her life (or mine) would look like 30 years later. We don't make decisions with foresight; we make them with whatever information is facing us at that moment. Life is a series of these 'in your face' decisions. In retrospect, I chose to have a life apart from Stephanie. I chose to immerse myself in work, to have a career, to pursue graduate degrees, to have a social life, to move to the country, to live in a beautiful place. I wanted my own identity. Selfish, some might say, and in many respects, they are right. Courageous, others might say, because I truly did want to put her needs first. At this point, however, it doesn't matter.

Stephanie is still mentally 2 ½ years of age but, amazingly, she continues to make progress. I expected her to plateau 40 years ago, but she still surprises us with new vocabulary, complete sentences, and logical responses. Recently, my sister and I were taking her home after a visit and I promised we would stop for some ice cream on the way. As we drove looking for an ice cream store, we passed McDonalds. Stephanie raised her hand and shouted "Donalds!" I asked, "What's at McDonalds, Stephanie?" thinking she would give her stock response of "hamburger, fries." Instead, "Ice cream!" she exclaimed – but the incredulous look on her face clearly said, *Duh*! We've always thought Stephanie had more going on in her brain than she was letting on. I hope she thinks I did well by her.

XXIII

MENTAL HEALTH

I wonder why the mention of heart disease or diabetes or cancer commands serious and important discussion but the mention of mental illness is cloaked in secrecy and shame. Still – in this day and age – with so much written on the subject and so many newsworthy people revealing their stories, how is it that I lowered my voice when I told friends I was going to be out of town because my son was in the throes of anxiety and needed me? They didn't ask questions and I appreciated their silence.

My mother admitted to suffering from "nerves" all her life, often taking to her bed, too weak to attend to daily chores and routine activities. In my childhood memories, I live with an angry, tired, and resentful mom. She seldom had energy to clean the house and I made excuses for keeping my friends out. She dreaded getting older and was perfectly fine with my telling everyone she was 29, for about five years in a row. When I showed her my engagement ring, she gave me a stoic, "Oh, he did it" and then procrastinated in helping me with wedding preparations. When I was in my early 40's, I disagreed with her (for the first time in my life) on some innocuous issue and, within minutes, she emptied out her hope chest of all my baby and childhood mementos and handed them to me in complete silence.

Today, we recognize these as signs of mental illness but it's still hard to utter the words. Harder for me is to acknowledge the periods in my life when I have felt slow-burning anger for reasons that were a mystery. Not that there weren't plenty of times when anger was more than justified. But anger with a cause and anger from depression *feel* different, don't they? One is targeted and meaningful; the other is generalized and debilitating. I anguish at the thought that I lashed out at my own children during these periods or, at the very least, wasn't very pleasant around them, causing them hurt.

I described in a previous chapter how Mom loved to tell the story of being taken to the doctor at the age of two because she was lethargic and didn't want to eat. The doctor told my grandparents to dress her in red and give in to her every whim. Initially, I thought Mom simply relished the memory of her father carrying her everywhere, but I now believe she was telling us she still needed to be carried, catered to, and protected. She desperately wanted to feel as safe and loved as she had in her father's arms.

I once asked Mom why I was afraid of the dark. I thought some traumatic experience in my childhood might explain it. She didn't hesitate in her answer, "I guess because I am." She didn't elaborate, but she didn't need to. She had always slept with a light in her bedroom. She was also afraid of loud noises, getting sick, being alone. My sister and I shouldn't wonder about our fears – we come by them legitimately. But I do wonder - does our anxiety make us fearful or do our fears make us anxious? At this point, it doesn't matter. Anxiety is ours to own whether it came in our genes or we learned it.

Stephanie is the one member of the family whose condition leans heavily on the side of nature in the nature vs. nurture debate. Doctors have been clear that her disability was present at the moment of conception. Still, there's no question environmental factors have influenced her. For example, she has mimicked the hand gestures, voice intonations and even verbal phrases of caregivers and staff over the years. But, her behavior is simple and reactive, not based on mental constructs like guilt or shame or painful memories.

Stephanie is on psychotropic medication for Bi Polar Disorder and Dysthymic Disorder (chronic depression). She sees a psychiatrist and a behavior specialist on a regular basis. She has been assessed as needing help with "noncompliance, physical aggression, throwing objects, and self-injurious behavior." Because of her mental limitations, these diagnoses have been reached, not by her describing how she feels or what she's thinking, but purely by her behavior and her response to medication. She still throws tantrums without (apparent) provocation, but is doing well within her stable environment.

My nephew, Juan, didn't have a chance at a stable environment. His dad, my brother, died before he was born and he was diagnosed as paranoid-schizophrenic in his late teens. He lived his entire adult life in mental health settings. I see Juan's diagnosis as the cruelest expression of nature and nurture. What might I be writing about him if he had been given a chance at whatever "normal" is? For Juan, his genetic makeup and his stormy childhood combined to deal him a tragic blow.

My own story is not tragic but is important to tell. I started "feeling funny" when my kids were young. The feeling is hard to describe but it was definitely both physical and mental – a warm sensation throughout my body and a sense of impending doom. It came out of nowhere, even when there was nothing to worry about. It didn't last long, maybe two or three hours, maybe three to five times a month. I remember thinking this must be what depression feels like but I didn't ascribe the condition to myself. It wasn't there when I was at work or otherwise distracted – only at home.

Separate from these episodes were longer periods when I just felt sad and angry, like the thread I was hanging on to was going to be snipped. To all outward appearances, I was functioning well but there was no joy in my life. I must have recognized this as depression, or at least as "nerves", because I took Mom-prescribed homeopathic remedies like Kali Phos.

Things improved in my 40's and 50's. My children were adults, my work responsibilities increased, I had a better sense of who I was as a person, and I looked forward to the future. I was managing the stresses in my life, those highs and lows that everyone experiences, and I would have described myself as "happy" had anyone asked. Then, five years after retirement, I met depression's other half – the flip side of the coin – anxiety.

In 2009, I suffered from severe back/chest pain that doctors ultimately diagnosed as *myofascial pain syndrome*. It felt like a dagger was permanently ensconced in the middle of my chest and the pain was equally unrelenting front and back. I woke up with it in the morning and I went to bed with it at night. My doctor referred me to physical therapy and, on my own, I saw a chiropractor who specialized in myofascial release and I tried acupuncture. Seven months into the pain, my doctor referred me to a rheumatologist to rule out any autoimmune condition. The rheumatologist said I didn't have anything she treated but suggested Tramadol, an opioid analgesic. NSAID pain relievers had not helped previously and I had resisted stronger forms of pain medication, but I was exhausted from the constant pain and agreed to try it.

My reaction was immediate. After the first dose, my scalp itched and I was drowsy. After the second dose, my life changed. I was sitting at the computer when suddenly a heavy wave of extreme anxiety broadsided me and knocked me off my feet. I was shocked, not knowing what hit me. It was both physical (a warm heaviness) and mental (a state of terror). The waves continued throughout the day. I found myself pacing around the deck like a caged animal and walking up the mountain behind the house trying to get away. Get away from what? I didn't know. I called the doctor and her nurse was reassuring. I didn't have to go to the ER, the reaction would not get any worse, and the Tramadol would be out of my system within 72 hours.

178

The 72 hours came and went and I wasn't better. I thought I was going crazy. If a doctor had offered to admit me into a psychiatric hospital, I would have gladly accepted. I thought of going to the ER and just sitting in the waiting room so that when something "bad" happened, I'd get help right away. But, I couldn't define what the "bad" was or imagine what the treatment might be. I was otherwise rational and knew I had to get help. If there was no longer any Tramadol in my system causing havoc, then there was a clear non-physical component to my problem, akin to people suffering continued physical pain after the cause of their pain has been resolved or people feeling pain in a limb that has been amputated. My pain, or in my case, anxiety, had taken on a life of its own. I quickly found a psychologist who practiced cognitive-behavioral therapy.

The psychologist offered guided imagery – a technique I had practiced in the past and with which I was comfortable. The sessions had the intended result of relaxation but two of them took us both by surprise. In one, I was to visualize walking into a warm body of water, going deeper and deeper until I was floating in peace. But in my mind, there was peril at every turn and I was sure I would be sucked under and drown. In the other session, I was to visualize walking in a beautiful area of meadows and pastures and woods. But in my mind, someone bad was lurking behind the trees ready to pounce and do me harm. There was no denying my deep-seated fears.

When my therapist suggested I deliberately bring on a wave of anxiety, I was horrified and told her so. Then she went one step further and proposed I embrace my anxiety. Why would I want to induce and then embrace the very thing I was trying to cure? She was right, or course, as I learned in the months that followed. The idea is to gain control over the anxiety; to have some say over when and how the wave hits; to take the power away from it; to own it. She had me repeat the mantra, "I welcome my anxiety and I embrace it." Unbelievable but I was eventually able to look my anxiety in the eye and defuse it. After six months of intensive therapy, when I tried to bring on a wave, I couldn't. The extreme anxiety was but a memory and I knew I could safely end the therapy.

I terminated physical therapy at about the same time. A year from onset, my back/chest pain was finally manageable. While we never determined the exact cause of my pain, the physical therapist observed that my body felt as though I had considerable scar tissue even though I had never had surgery. She believed the periods of severe stress in my life had produced the same effect.

By no means have I seen an end to all pain and anxiety. These, I'm afraid, will be lifelong companions. At least once a week, I feel a gripping sensation as though someone is massaging my heart. But, it only lasts a minute or less and I'm no longer afraid of it. I also still have periods of anxiety but nothing like the waves of the past. I'm most susceptible to anxiety and panic in the middle of the night. I imagine the worst possible catastrophes and go to the darkest of places. Sometimes, I have to get out of bed to pace around my bedroom while taking deep breaths. I have a toolbox of anti-anxiety weapons: a night light, of course; a lighthearted program on television (*I Love Lucy* at 3:00 am does wonders); playing a game on my phone (*7 Little Words* and *Spider Solitaire* are my favorite); reciting the rosary (usually asleep by the fourth decade); and singing a *Jesus* song (to myself, naturally). Meditation doesn't work for me at night because it's too easy for my mind to wander back into dark thoughts.

The war rages on but I believe I'm winning important battles. First, I take personal responsibility for what's happening to my body and mind. This means looking at alternative (as well as conventional) forms of treatment, taking seriously the role of diet and exercise in maintaining health, and making a commitment to myself to get better. No going to a doctor or therapist expecting (s)he will fix me; no taking a pill expecting it to do all the work; no feeling sorry for myself. There is nothing easy about this – this is hard work and it's for me to do.

During the year I fought constant pain and severe anxiety, no one outside my family would have guessed anything was wrong. I got up every morning, looked at my calendar, and did what had to be done. I went to yoga and circuit-training classes, participated in church activities, and ran all the normal errands of daily life. I drove to Southern California for my father's funeral. I even accepted and took part in a demanding County/State project that included meetings, interviews, group functions, and a lot of writing. I also broke my foot that year, hobbling around on a therapeutic boot and requiring more physical therapy.

A side benefit of all this activity was my discovery that distraction is a wonderful friend. Whether you're involved in a meaningful activity, playing a game, or walking around the mall, you're forced to think outside yourself and focus on something besides your pain. The pain is still there but it takes a back seat to the other activity. I'm grateful for this discovery and now when I start to feel bad, I get up and *do* something.

How much you should do and when you should do it are not always easy to gauge, however. When Margaret, was 11, she told me she was tired of breathing. I was taken aback and wanted to know more. She didn't have more to tell – only that she could feel every breath she took and sometimes she got tired of it. I was shaken but rationalized there was plenty going on in the family that might upset a little girl. We had just gone though a grueling divorce and the tension had not yet abated. Margaret, at such a young age, was responsible for helping me care for developmentally delayed Stephanie. And, to top it off, her brothers were giving her a hard time, as older brothers are apt to do.

I decided she was going to be all right; she just needed a break outside the house. We deserved quiet time together, just the two of us, to kick back and talk. This was the beginning of many trips (mostly long weekends) over the next few years to the Channel Islands/Port Hueneme area of Ventura in which Margaret and I played on the beach, ate pizza, and lounged around. It was perfect and I thought her "tired of breathing" problem had been resolved; at the least, she had never complained about it again.

About 25 years later, I'm sitting next to Margaret at her doctor's office. Margaret has lost a tremendous amount of weight and she's talking about her suicidal overtures; her attempts to curb her mental pain by inflicting physical pain through burning of her body and tattooing. The doctor asks when her mental anguish started and Margaret begins with, "When I was 11...."

I felt as though struck by lightning. Could I have changed the course of Margaret's depression and anxiety by taking her early complaints more seriously? Should I have rushed her to a psychologist or psychiatrist? Was I completely naïve to think I could solve a cry for help with a trip to the beach? I don't think Margaret blames me. But...I do blame myself.

While Margaret's depression led her to inflict physical pain on herself, Vincent's severe panic disorder leads him to mental agony. He goes deep into his soul in search of "sins" that tell him he is not deserving of anything good. Then he is consumed by guilt and shame. Even as a child, Vincent was ready to beat himself up – literally. When he was about seven, he accidentally slammed a door on Christopher's finger (cutting off the tip) and was inconsolable as he cried and hit his arms with his fists.

Vincent's panic attacks can last a few days or a few months. What I admire most is his tenacity in looking for help and his resolve to get there. In the midst of mental torment, he will search for the right doctor and the right treatment. He doesn't settle. When a psychiatrist offered him heavy-duty prescriptions after a 20-minute consultation, Vince never returned. When he had two therapists that he liked, he talked to both. I saw him return from a run and collapse on the floor; then do the run again, every day. He practiced Qigong even though it was painful. He had acupuncture and drank a most unappetizing Chinese tea. He regularly visited an osteopath in Montebello and then found an osteopath in Fresno (he lived in the Central Valley at the time) who specialized in psychiatric services. These doctors helped Vincent immensely but I truly believe it was Vince's persistent efforts that set the foundation for any healing that has taken place.

The journey continues for Vince. The lesson to learn from him is this: You are the expert of your mind and body. No one else can tell you what is best for you. You have to be your own advocate. You have to dig deep, explore every possibility, and never give up. I've said it before and Vincent confirms it: this is hard work and only you can do it, for however long it takes and as many times as it takes.

None of my children or grandchildren has escaped some form and some degree of depression or anxiety. Michael and Christopher delayed facing their demons through self-medication. Mike now manages his by throwing himself into work and Chris focuses on literary outlets. For both of them, their music is their therapy and distraction. Heather is open about her feelings and reaches out to family and friends. Andrew shares his pain easily and aspires to help others through the journey. Sarah still struggles with the burden placed upon her as a child to be the "parent." Vance is quiet on the subject and prefers privacy.

In a conference many years ago, the speaker asked participants to think about their greatest fear in life. I had no trouble with that. My lifelong fear had been *to be found out* – to be recognized as a phony; not as smart or as good or as anything positive as anyone believed. I had been able to fool those around me into thinking I was a capable, sensitive, reasonably intelligent person, but the day would come (maybe tomorrow) when I would be seen as a complete fake and the truth would humiliate me. I spent my days looking over my shoulder, second-guessing myself, waiting for the inevitable.

During a family barbeque 25 years later, the conversation came to center around the many mental health problems that assault our family. During that barbeque, I discovered that *fear of being found out* was a common thread among my family members. In fact, I didn't introduce the subject but, as soon as it was mentioned, there were echoes of "me too" even from Sarah who epitomizes self-confidence. I was sad that so many of us had lifelong doubts about our abilities, but that is just another side effect of depression. It robs you of your identity and self-esteem and chips away at your core till you're not sure who you really are.

That family event stands out in my mind as a turning point, an afternoon of discovery and healing. Vincent shared his experiences with severe anxiety and the others followed. Depression, anxiety, doubt, fear, pain – everyone opened up with personal stories and we were stunned by their similarities. What was most gratifying to me was the support and love offered by each individual to all the others. No one was alone that evening. We were a family.

Right after the family barbeque, Christopher suggested we create a text system by which family members could continue reaching out and supporting one another. Within days, Sarah used the WhatsApp application to construct a group called Family Support. Immediately, responses started pouring in. Margaret said we "need to hear what needs to be said and then love and comfort each other....with no judgment." Heather was "glad we have this so we can be open with each other."

Family members described what they felt when hit by depression or anxiety: "an empty abyss without any end....itchy, crawling, painful sensations on skin....hate the phone....mind can't function....something attacking me....chest is heavy...."

They also offered tips remarkably similar to what my psychologist had given me many years prior: "name it....don't give it power....don't be afraid of it....tell yourself it's not your fault...."

The Family Support chat line has become our lifeline. We use it to let family members know when we're having a rough time, to offer ideas that might help, to announce good things in our lives, and to let off steam. The notices and the responses are immediate and from the heart. Andrew is always reassuring and compassionate. Heather recently wrote, "...you guys always help bring me back." But my favorite lines belong to Christopher: "I truly thought I was the weirdo of the family. But now I feel almost normal in our collective weirdness."

A few days after the debut of the family chat line, Chris sent out this poem:

TOGETHER WE CAN DO IT

To wake up and know
 the day is already over
What do you do with that
 there's no where to go

To open your eyes and know
 That life has nothing for you
Maybe if we wait a while
 Stay here and hide, let time tell

To enter the day and know
 there's no way you're gonna make it
The games you play are all the same
 It's only for so long that one can take it

A non-life is what they'd call it
 (If they only knew)
That's not living,
 dying or anything
This is purely
 non-existence

So close your swollen eyes and know
 it's time to ride the darkened horse
A wasted life is a waste of life
 the bleeding heart beats with remorse

To stab the unlovable soul
 with contempt
And divide the pieces among the
 wretched and begging
I guess I'm what's left

    TOGETHER

To face the empty page and know
 there's always somewhere safe to go
Where good, bad, happy and sad,
 alive or dead, is all in your head

A broken place with a door to escape
 a few degrees off from a tweak here or there
A body could get lost in a mind so creative
 it's not about pain and torturous despair

To stare at the half eaten mind and know
 it's a madness that will never end
Words drip from the bloody edge of my sword
 I'll flip your fucking lid with the tip of my pen

A bad trip, that's what it is
 (if they only knew)
That's not writing,
 dying or anything
That is surely
 deep indulgence

To fix the frustrated phrase with intent
 the day destroys the unbearable night
Another chance to laugh out loud & write it down
 and make everything appear to be alright
                                    Again

To wrap the uncontrollable soul
 in contentment
Unite through creative, artistic expression
 I think that's what I'm meant to be

    WE CAN DO IT!!

XXIV

DEATH

Expected or unexpected, there's no good way to do it. Not for the person who's dying and not for the loved ones left behind. It wasn't meant to be easy – didn't Jesus cry when he learned of Lazarus' death? Oh, I'm sure there have been those lucky few who have lived long, healthy lives and then died peacefully surrounded by loving family. Physically and mentally healthy to the end with a quick and un-dramatic exit – that's my idea of a good death. But, so far, that has not been my experience.

There was one more Juan in the family who died tragically – Juan Perea, son of my aunt and uncle, Lola and Sotero. Like my brother, Juan Perea was also the victim of an accident and was six days shy of his 21st birthday at the time of his death on June 22, 1981. This is my personal recollection of events: Juan was involved in a head-on collision on a busy street close to the family home. It appeared that he died instantly. Friends who witnessed the accident recognized that Juan was involved and notified Lola and Sotero immediately. Because a fatality was involved, no one could disturb the scene until the Coroner's Office arrived and completed their preliminary investigation, so the parents were remanded to their car as they waited and watched (possibly for hours). I can't imagine the agony and it tears me apart every time I think about it.

I remember being in awe of Lola during the funeral services. I knew she had to be completely devastated, but she remained calm and composed throughout the ordeal. She reminded me of my mother and sister-in-law who had shown such strength when my brother, Juan, died. Mom, however, was unable to attend Juan Perea's funeral. She shut down completely at the news of his death and was physically unable to get out of bed. And, my sister-in-law, who had been so strong when my brother died, was sobbing outside of church at Juan Perea's funeral. Likewise, Lola, who was now the pillar of strength, was inconsolable a short time later when Nani (her mother) died. There is no question that the effects of grief are cumulative. As we experience subsequent deaths, the new pain simply layers on top of previous pain and we mourn them all collectively – again.

My grandmother, Nani, died in 1975 at the age of 78, a good age for a woman of her generation. But many of those later years were painful to watch. Nani was an active, vibrant woman as I was growing up and I hold the happiest memories of her. But, that's not true for many of my cousins who experienced her as an aging and increasingly unpleasant person. We didn't know much about dementia in those days and Alzheimer's was not part of our vocabulary. We simply considered senility a natural consequence of old age and gave little consideration to the special needs of the old or the very special needs of their caregivers.

Nani lived with Lola and her family for most of her latter years. Except for talk of arthritis and an occasional mention of hardening of the arteries, I don't remember that Nani had many physical ailments. However, sometime in her 60's she required a wheelchair and then began to deteriorate quickly. It may have been in her very early 70's that she entered a nursing home located directly across the street from Lola and Sotero's home. Lola continued to nurse Nani, visiting her multiple times a day, helping her dress and assisting with feeding. Mom was there often also, maybe daily, and Hilda (who lived further away) visited as often as she could.

I don't remember going to the nursing home more than a handful of times. How is that possible, I ask? I was less than 40 minutes away and I cherished my Nani. My rationale is that I was maxed out coping with a difficult home situation and a demanding job; in other words, I was doing the best I could. That doesn't make me feel any better today. The truth is I hated the look and the feel and the smell of the nursing home and, when Nani no longer knew who I was, I didn't want to see her. I believe in doing the right thing, whether it feels good or not. In this instance, I didn't do the right thing.

The death of an old person is sad, of course, but mourning consists mostly of reliving memories of that person – conversations, experiences, relationships, etc. But…what about babies? Babies who die before, during, or soon after birth? That grief is unfathomable because what started out as joyful anticipation turns into the ultimate loss – loss of your own flesh and blood to love, loss of your identity as a parent, loss of a lifetime of potential memories.

Cousin Pilar conceived a baby girl in the late 70's. In her seventh month, or so, she had a vivid dream that Nani (our grandmother) came to take the baby with her. Pilar knew immediately her baby was no longer alive and this was confirmed by her doctor the following day. Labor was induced and Pilar gave birth to Cruzita (named after Nani) who was stillborn. Pilar has five sons who she adores but her baby girl has a special place in her (and our) heart.

In 1988, Cousin Ana knew for two months that the baby boy she was carrying would die soon after birth. An ultrasound following a minor auto accident revealed that Paul Ignacio Ogaz had anencephaly, a serious birth defect in which the top of a baby's head does not form properly. Ana was offered the option of a therapeutic abortion but refused. Baby Paul lived for six hours. All funerals are sad, but Baby Paul's was haunting, as we all stood numb and in complete silence after the gravesite services, not knowing what to do next.

There may have been other miscarriages in the family but I only know of two. Cousin Sonia and granddaughter Heather both lost babies early in their pregnancies, before knowing their gender. Both had been thrilled to be pregnant. Heather's mother had travelled to be with her daughter at this happy time. Heather suffered emotionally and grieves her profound loss to this day. Sonia went on to have three healthy children, but the pain of the first baby doesn't go away.

I was most fortunate to have lived for 29 years without losing anyone close to me. I had a relatively carefree childhood and loved growing up surrounded by extended family. Having my Nani and my aunts and uncle in the back house made me feel safe. Until they married and left the house (and even beyond that), Lola, Hilda and Ramiro always had time for me and tended to my woes no matter how slight or silly. And, when each died, a little piece of my heart went with them.

Ramiro, the baby of the family, died first, in 1984, at the age of 52. He had his first heart attack in his 40's and it left him with permanent coronary damage. He did not survive his second attack. Ramiro fought in the Korean War and had most certainly returned with Post Traumatic Stress Disorder, although it was not a recognized medical condition at the time. He had terrible nightmares and may have attempted to self-medicate with alcohol. When my brother Juan died, Ramiro fell apart. I remember my aunt, Gloria, driving him to Mom and Pops' house and Ramiro being unable to get out of the car, doubled over with grief. Between sobs he asked why Juan had to die when he, himself, had been spared.

Lola, who died in 2008 at the age of 83, succumbed to the ravages of Alzheimer's. When my mother was dying, Lola came to the house daily to talk with Mom, read with her, pray with her, and hold her hand. She was a rock in the midst of chaos. I needed that. Then, to watch her slip away – slowly, insidiously, unrelentingly, was devastating. When I moved up North in 1999 and until January 2001, she wrote letters and sent me cheery cards, giving me the family news and sometimes complaining about her shakiness and forgetfulness. When I saw her at my uncle George's funeral, she threw her arms around me with joy and I was struck by her child-like manner. In 2003, when I went South to my grandson Andrew's high school graduation, I stayed the night at Lola and Sotero's house. She knew who I was and was delighted to see me but couldn't remember anything about my current circumstances and asked me where I lived over and over again. When I left in the morning, she was washing clothes and glared at me as though I was a total stranger. The next time I saw her, she was in her own space, completely unreachable and unresponsive. I give her children and my uncle, Sotero, my everlasting admiration for lovingly taking care of her and allowing her the dignity to die in her own bed.

Hilda, who I think of as the spunky one, remained in character to the end. My uncle, George, died in September of 2001, just following the terrorist attack of 9/11. He had been diagnosed with congestive heart failure a few years earlier and died quietly in the early morning with Hilda sleeping nearby. Uncharacteristically for our family and despite pleas from her children, Hilda was determined to live alone in the large, rambling family home. All went fairly well until 2009 when she had unexpected surgery for a clogged right femoral artery followed by a series of complications. At one rehabilitation center, her wound became infected and she required another surgery to remove the affected tissue. She ended up with a 10-inch incision that included her entire thigh.

I saw Hilda in a nursing home in November when she appeared to be well on the road to recovery. She was her usual bubbly, loquacious self as she introduced me to staff. She had had her hair fixed and had bragged to anyone who would listen that her niece was coming from up North to visit her. She was also a bit snippy, rolling her eyes when the doctor told her to exercise and refusing to fully cooperate with physical therapy. That was Hilda, unapologetic about her feelings. She was able to return home for a short while only to become ill again. She was subsequently diagnosed with Non-Hodgkin's lymphoma and was placed on a respirator. Her children had the heartbreaking task of having her taken off life-support and Hilda died peacefully a half hour later on April 14, 2010 at the age of 80.

When a child dies, the grief is unrelenting and torturous. When loved ones die, the grief is targeted albeit cumulative. When a parent dies, the grief is complicated. Whether you are holding your parent's hand or oceans away; whether your relationship was close or distant; whether your memories are comforting or distressing; whether the death was lingering or a surprise – it's still your mom or dad and grief becomes entangled with guilt and remorse and relief and numbness and utter sadness.

Mom became sick in April of 1996 – a cold that turned into a cough and then into a lingering malaise. At first, her lack of energy and appetite did not particularly concern us because this had been a pattern most of her life. But as weeks turned into months, Sonia (who lived with our parents and was their provider and caregiver) became alarmed and asked me to help keep an eye on Mom. Sonia worked full time, was planning her wedding to Miguel, and made occasional trips to Maryland where Miguel lived. I was on summer vacation from school and worked sporadically and mostly from home, so I could do it.

As I spent time with Mom, I became more aware of her increasing lethargy, her fastidious reaction toward food, and her chronic cough. Although she looked away disgustingly any time I mentioned going to the doctor, I finally just made the appointment, put her in the car, and took her in. It was August 26, 1996. She answered the doctor's questions in a lighthearted manner and minimized her symptoms. The cough was "almost gone" she said. I interrupted every answer and forced my own opinion, looking, I'm sure, like the overbearing daughter.

The chest x-ray showed fluid in her lungs. The doctor removed it but fluid immediately filled her lungs again. Mom was terrified. Her worst nightmare was to be hospitalized (Sonia spent one night in the hospital with her and I spent the next). Sonia mentioned her approaching wedding and honeymoon to one of the doctors who said Mom had been sick for a long time but would "probably still be with us" when Sonia returned from her honeymoon. Sonia and I were stunned. We knew Mom was very sick but it had never occurred to us that she might die. Shortly after that conversation, an MRI confirmed the diagnosis: lung cancer.

The doctor was relaxed and precise as she gave us the news. There was nothing to be done – Mom would die of the cancer – it could take two weeks or two years. Mom reacted with concern for everyone else. Pops didn't blink as he took it all in. Frank, Linda and I stayed strong because it was the thing to do. My nephew, Michael, and niece, Melissa, played noisily in the hallway outside the hospital room.

Mom was desperate to leave the hospital but there was a delay because she still had a draining tube in her chest. When I threatened to take her out of the hospital AMA (against medical advice) the doctor came running and removed the drain. We had a wedding to attend and little time to get ready.

Sonia and Miguel got married at Mt. Tabor Monastery in Ukiah on August 31, 1996, three days after Mom was discharged. Hilda stayed with Mom and Pops while the rest of us travelled to Ukiah. Things were happening very fast with no time to process anything, but it was clear that Mom was shocked that Sonia had proceeded with the wedding and was going off to honeymoon in Italy. She had assumed (probably since she first got sick) that all such plans would be cancelled. When Sonia called her after the wedding, Mom didn't want to talk with her. Hilda made her take the phone.

As soon as I returned home, I moved into Mom and Pops' house. I was there all week, going home only on Saturday and returning the following day. Linda came every day after dropping the kids off at school and stayed until it was time to pick them up. Then on Saturday, the whole family (Frank, Linda, Michael, Melissa) came and stayed overnight so I could have some respite. It was a grueling schedule for all of us. I can't imagine trying to do it alone.

Thank God for hospice. An amazing nurse visited often; a social worker was always on stand-by; and when the time came, a hospital bed was set up and a gentle caregiver dropped in to bathe her and change her bedding. Mom had resisted the idea of Hospice initially but then agreed because they offered to keep her from being hospitalized again. Still, she was brusque and never had a kind word for any of them.

Mom had always been in control of her environment and of those around her. I say this simply to describe her, not to judge her. She was a manipulative woman and throughout my life had used illness, physical weakness and "nerves" to achieve this control. It did not cease simply because she had come to the end of her life. Whenever Sonia called, Mom sounded wretched even if she had been fine just before taking the phone. She needed sympathy that, unfortunately, she wasn't getting from me. I had control issues of my own and it was one strong will against the other.

If this was a competition, Mom was winning. She demanded that someone be at her side at all times. If I needed to use the bathroom and Pops was working in the yard, I'd have to call him in before I could leave her room. She ran me and Pops and Linda ragged as we tried to fix her something she could eat – running back and forth to the kitchen as she rejected item after item because it was too hot or cold, gritty or slimy, lumpy or soft. I slept in a fold-away bed next to her hospital bed and the demands continued all night. She'd insist that I hold her hand, which meant I couldn't recline on the bed and therefore couldn't sleep. I caught snatches of sleep by pretending that I didn't see her outstretched hand, only to deal with the guilt in the morning. I asked the Hospice nurse if I was running a sprint or a marathon because if it was a marathon, I wasn't going to make it.

I survived by creating a separate environment that I could control. Every morning, I looked around the house and found a section of closet or a set of drawers or other cluttered space that I could work on that day (if outside Mom's bedroom, I worked at it during the hours Linda was there). If by the end of the day the closet or drawers or space was cleared or neatly organized, then I declared it a good day. I desperately needed something with a beginning and an end that was observably productive (and satisfied my OCD needs). There was also an unexpected benefit. As I was de-cluttering the house, I found several stashes of cash neatly hidden in pouches and leather billfolds, up to $700 at a time. There was also the odd $50 or $100 bill carefully placed in a book or envelope. I didn't dare throw anything away without thoroughly inspecting it. Linda and I were able to open a bank account for Mom's funeral expenses and, in the end, she paid for a large portion of her own services.

Mom wasn't ready to die. She wanted a healing, a miracle. She asked that Fr. John Hampsch (a healing priest with the Charismatic Renewal) come to the house to pray over her. I was able to reach him and he offered to pray with her over the phone. She was furious when I handed the phone to her and hardly listened to his prayer. She was angry – with everything, at everyone, but mostly angry with God. How could He allow this to happen? She wanted her miracle and appeared to never reconcile with the fact that she was dying.

Frank tried to give Mom her miracle. He heard of a Chinese doctor who could diagnose someone by just looking at them and then offer miraculous cures. Frank made an appointment and we took Mom to see him but the news was not good. The doctor said the cancer was "all over" her body and all he could do was give her something to provide some peace and comfort. We tried the various teas and the shark cartilage he recommended but Mom said she couldn't swallow them.

Mom died on November 6, 1996, a little over two months after diagnosis. It was a pretty good death, really. She was never in any pain and didn't have the shortness of breath that comes with lung cancer. She never took as much as an aspirin and allowed the oxygen only because the nurse insisted. Towards the end, she spent a lot of time drawn inwardly and then stopped eating altogether. The only visible sign of impending death was the purple color of her feet and the fact she felt no cold. She always appeared to understand what was going on around her; in fact, the morning she died the nurse offered to catheterize her because she had not urinated and Mom opened eyes, looked right at her and said emphatically, "Don't do it!"

The day Mom died, the Hospice nurse brought along a new nurse she was training and the two of them were working at the dining room table. Our nurse had alerted us that death was imminent and I had notified Sonia. Linda and I were standing by Mom's bed just watching her breathe when the breaths became erratic. Linda quickly got Pops who was working outside and I called the nurses. Mom took her last breath with Pops, Linda, the two nurses and me around the bed. The Hospice nurse called the time of death while the nurse in training softly cried as she witnessed her first death on the job. They then called the mortuary but asked them not to take the body until Frank got home to say his good-byes.

It was a little over two months between diagnosis and death. Mom wasn't in pain and was rational and clear-headed. I was by her side 24/7. It was a perfect time to ask lingering questions, reconcile past issues, express final I love you's. It didn't happen. Mom was angry and unyielding, looking away and uttering, "Whatever God wants" with a shake of her head and the lift of an eyebrow. I was angry and unyielding, too, and refused to beg for her attention. It wasn't until the night before she died that I said the rosary and sang "Alleluia" to her as she came in and out of awareness. Too little, too late, I think.

When we took Mom to the Chinese doctor, we asked him to take a look at Pops as he sat waiting, completely unaware he was being assessed. The doctor took one look at him and laughed. "He's going to live a long time," he said. Well, the doctor was right. Pops died in November of 2009 at the age of 94. He just wasted away, physically and mentally. Whereas Mom's death had been fast and furious, Pops' death was slow and tedious.

When Mom died, Pops talked about "going to my honey" as though it would happen the next day. He talked to her picture every night and reassured her that he was coming and would see her soon. But when a year passed and he was still on earth, he decided if he was going to live, then he should *really* live. For the next several years, he accepted every travel opportunity with Sonia and Miguel, referring to them as his adventures: a cruise to Alaska, a helicopter flight over the Grand Canyon, a trip to Niagara Falls, and jaunts to New York, Atlanta and Columbia, South America. When I moved up North, he thoroughly enjoyed visiting me summers – watching the deer and squirrels, exploring the woods, and even pulling weeds. He talked about how fortunate he was to be able to spend time with each of his children. He lived with Frank and Linda, visited me, and travelled with Sonia and Miguel. He boasted that life was good!

Between age 85 and 90, Pops found his voice and began to express his thoughts and feelings (something he didn't do while married). We had real conversations. We found that he had political and social opinions. He even started worrying – a job previously held by Mom. We also (for the first time) saw his stubborn side – the side that vociferously objected to senior day care until they asked him not to return; the side that complained when left home alone but declined every invitation to go out; the side that refused to wash his hands after using the restroom and before eating ("look, they're clean!"). Bathing became the topic of many animated discussions and it's only been very recently that I understand how simple things like taking a shower can be a really big deal.

When we celebrated Pops' 90th birthday, he was still physically strong and mentally alert. The decline then began, slowly but steadfastly. When he asked whether Frank was his brother or his son, we knew he had taken a turn. When he couldn't remember Lola's funeral two days after the event, we placed ourselves on alert. As Pops turned 93, Sonia and Miguel took him to live with them and I provided short bits of respite so they could travel. It wasn't long before Pops lost all memory and thought he was living in a facility with us as staff. "I hope you're getting overtime," he told me one evening and "I want to see the manager of this place," he demanded when he was unhappy with something I had done. Thank God for John Wayne westerns and *Bonanza* that provided snatches of entertainment for him and relief for us.

The anger and the paranoia were the hardest parts of his illness. Pops became increasingly demanding and expressed his rage by yelling and banging on the walls, sure he was being held captive and insisting he be allowed to go home. When I asked where "home" was he always said Douglas, Arizona where he was born. I became angry, too, when he called for me all night long. Sleep deprivation is a terrible thing. Then there was the time he fell at about 3:00 in the morning as he transitioned himself from his portable potty to the bed and I had to call 911 for help getting him up. Six big, burly guys walked into the bedroom and Pops was delighted to see them, as though they were there for a party.

A few months before Pops died, Sonia bit the bullet and found a nursing home for him. He was confused initially but eventually settled in and was comfortable. How nice to be able to get up in the middle of the night for a yogurt without disrupting anyone's sleep. Pops even flirted with the nurses as Mom, I'm sure, turned over in her grave. On November 15, 2009, Pops passed away quietly while Sonia, Miguel and Margaret were on their way to see him. When they walked into his room, Tumbleweed (Margaret's large chocolate lab) jumped up on the bed with him, much to Sonia's surprise and Margaret's delight. Pops was cremated and his ashes were laid next to Mom's casket.

Since I originally wrote this reflection, two more members of the family have passed away. On October 26, 2015, David Avila (cousin Hilda's husband) died of a massive heart attack at the young age of 57. We are again reminded we can never take life for granted. One morning, David kisses his wife good-by as he leaves for work and by evening she is a widow and three young adults are without their dad. Death does come like a stranger in the night.

But.....not always. At age 94, Uncle Sotero Perea's death was well anticipated when on July 3, 2016, he passed peacefully at home, surrounded by children and grandchildren. Despite a history of cardiac problems, Sotero was remarkably healthy as he took care of my aunt Lola during her lingering illness. And, he stayed strong until the two weeks before he died. Of all the deaths in the family thus far, his is the one I would choose for myself.

I'm not afraid of death, but I am afraid of the process of dying. If death means the glory of heaven, or even if it is just the state of nothingness, I will probably welcome it. But the course and the manner of dying terrifies me. This is largely because I'm a person who wants to know how things will go. I'm not a play-it-by-ear person or a let's-see-how-it-goes person. I'm a plan-every-detail-so-I'll-know-exactly-how-it-will-go person. And with benefit of the internet, that's pretty doable. Except for dying. That's the one activity you can't plan, dictate, rehearse for, or duplicate if the first time doesn't go well. That's the one event you can't influence with wealth, education, prestige, power or authority. It doesn't care if you or your loved ones are ready. It comes when it comes, and there's nothing you can do about it.

I don't think of myself as a controlling person but, of course, I am. I have absolutely no desire to control other people but I definitely want to control my own environment. I want my things neatly organized my way. I apologize now to my children and grandchildren for any unpleasantness on my part when I'm old and they're trying to help. I'm doing all I can to avoid the need for any of my progeny to have to put up with me as I age. I have a little long-term-care insurance and would welcome a nursing home rather than being a burden to my family. And, make no mistake, I will be a burden to any relative trying to care for me. I believe that as people age, their peculiarities do also. I will be dictating every move around me. Trust me, you don't want that!

Since it's my death we're reflecting on, I want a say in it. I've done everything that can be done ahead of time. I have a living will. I have a binder with information for my children on all my accounts and insurances. I have funeral and burial instructions. But unfortunately for people like me, only the ancillary activities can be planned. The questions I have about dying itself will not be answered until my time comes. Will I suffer? Will I be physically incapacitated or mentally impaired? Will I be angry and ugly or mean? Will I make life difficult for my family? Will I linger, wishing death would hurry? The thought of lying on a bed unable to breathe easily or move about freely throws me into a panic. That's because my worst fear since I was about eight years of age has been to be buried alive. (At that time, I read about a girl my age who had been kidnapped and subsequently buried alive and I completely identified with her.) So, the mere thought of being restricted or confined can trigger an anxiety attack. I hope my children have the courage to let me go quickly and, even, to hasten the end in whatever way is legally available. While I remain pro-life, I believe it would be moral for me to provide a nudge to my own inevitable outcome. Please don't extend my life by protracting my death.

They say that when you look back on your life, you don't regret the things you did; you regret the things you didn't do. What I regret most is never learning to speak Spanish really well. When I worked and carried Spanish-speaking cases, I was able to communicate with clients in a rudimentary, vernacular Spanish. But when I was contacted by someone in the Mexican consulate or the Spanish-speaking media, I was tongue-tied. Spanish was my first language and I'm embarrassed to say that I can hardly get a coherent sentence out now.

If I had written the script of my life, I would have made every important decision with the clarity only hindsight offers. But that's not how it goes. We live our lives amidst uncertainties and challenges, making amends for past wrongs and hoping for better tomorrows. Tomorrow, however, has a mind of its own and so all we really have is right now, this moment. My life has had more joyful and satisfying moments than sad or disappointing ones. For that I am very grateful.

ACKNOWLEDGEMENTS

I offer my deepest gratitude to:

Lenore Dowling, IHM, who taught me to write in the eighth grade by covering my work with red markings.

Anita Kemp, Ph.D., without whose focus I would not have conceived how to start my writing.

Debra Ginsberg, for her helpful editing and her encouraging words when I needed them most.

Marilyn Kilpatrick, for calming my fears and taking the intimidation out of the printing process.

Linda Miles, for patiently unraveling the mysteries of digital technology, thus keeping me sane.

Taryn Evans, for enthusiastically working her magic on my challenging photographs.

And especially my flawed yet extraordinary family, for allowing me to bring their stories to life because as my eldest son said, "the truth is the truth."

Nani and Grandfather
She, barely out of her teens
He, twelve years older.

Mom and Lola with Nachito
who died at age two
probably during flu epidemic.

Mom and Me
Even our curls match.

"Papy" and Me
Hanging out with my dad
In Douglas, Arizona.

Nani, always my refuge.
Uncle Ramiro, more like a big brother.

Aunt Lola
Sensible, practical,
loved her infectious laugh.

Aunt Hilda
Vivacious, carefree,
ready to take me under her wing.

Lola and Hilda, toiling on wash day
as we all did prior to clothes dryers.

Sonia and I peek through the
door window and enjoy Juan's antics
in Ramiro's boots.

Typical Nani
Comforting Juan with one hand,
scratching the dog with the other.

First Holy Communion,
an important event in the life of a
Catholic family in the 40's.

Sonia, Juan and me, dressed in
traditional Mexican attire and ready
to enjoy the church *Jamaica*.

The family at the beach, that means everybody .
Starting with male on the far left and going clockwise:
Ramiro, me, Pops (standing), Lola, unidentified friend,
Hilda helping Sonia, Nani (lying down).
Mom must have taken the picture.

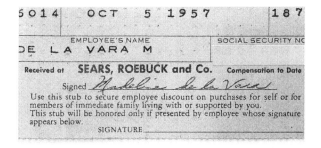

I started working at Sears , Roebuck and Co.
the summer before my senior year in high school and
through the end of my sophomore year in college.
Jobs were plentiful in department stores and
any 16 or 17-year old who wanted to work could.
No online shopping back then.

I would have started working one year earlier;
however, when Paco was born
I became his full time second mother.
No surprise we were frolicking in the park 2 years later.

Throwing the wedding bouquet
at our backyard potluck reception.

And seven years later....

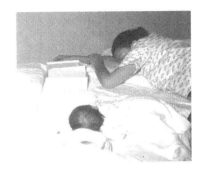

Sleeping with Michael.

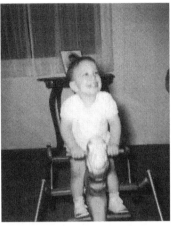

Vincent enjoying his horse.

Stephanie at eight months.

Christopher, a joy to be around.

Enjoying the backyard.
Chris studying Stephanie.
Mike and Vince content.

Margaret doing her own thing.

Rare photo of me with all five kids:
Christopher, Michael, Vincent, Margaret standing
Stephanie with me in front.

Heather with me at work
for Christmas party.

Heather, brief but
spectacular equestrian.

Andrew
Adorable from the start.

Andrew with me relaxing in back yard
as Vincent looks on.

Sarah and Vance at
horseback riding lesson.

At the petting zoo
Sarah was gentle
but the animals were never
the same after Vance left.

Sarah, determined
even though piñata and stick are both
bigger than she is.

Easter egg hunts can be
challenging
but Sarah knows just how they go.

UCLA Sculpture Garden
Sarah is curious but discreet
Vance wants to explore further.
My fantasy has always been that Sarah would attach
copies of these photos to her application
to graduate school at UCLA.

My car with peace sign,
against nuclear weapons.

Favorite pastime – hiking,
here in the Austrian Alps.

Stephanie, happy
as she plays on swing
and listens to music.

Nephew Juan brought new meaning
to the expression *hanging from the
chandelier* – or in this case,
the door jamb.

Juan Dela Vara
1970 - 2006

JUAN NICOLAS DELA VARA
1948 - 1970

Made in the USA
Columbia, SC
10 July 2018